REAL
HEROES
OF THE
OLD TESTAMENT

REAL HEROES
OF THE
OLD TESTAMENT

LORI L. DENNING

CFI
An imprint of Cedar Fort, Inc.
Springville, Utah

ISBN 13: 978-1-4621-4285-9

Published by CFI, an imprint of Cedar Fort, Inc.
2373 W. 700 S., Springville, UT 84663
Distributed by Cedar Fort, Inc., www.cedarfort.com

Library of Congress Control Number: 2022933513

Cover design by Courtney Proby
Cover design © 2022 Cedar Fort, Inc.

Printed in the United States of America

10 9 8 7 6 5 4 3 2 1

Printed on acid-free paper

For Diane

CONTENTS

ACKNOWLEDGMENTS

I stand on the backs of giants—spiritual giants, scholarly giants, and genuinely amazing Saints.

I am nothing without my dear family. My dad taught me how to work hard. There is no substitute for hard work and an honest day's effort. My mom taught me how to be friendly and the importance of schoolwork. Her kindness is contagious, and she is everyone's friend and confidant. Eternally she is my supporter and cheerleader. She also insisted I learn keyboarding—a gift that keeps on giving. My brother Mike taught me how to relate to people from all walks of life. From surfboards to boardrooms, Mike understands people. My brother Rick taught me to be a disciple. Rick always does the right thing and follows the Lord. My twin, Lisa, led me to love scripture and literature. She taught me to laugh and love. She also taught me many things I may have had to unlearn over the years, but I am sworn to secrecy as wonder-twins.

My best friend, Diane, is the best at humility. She is kind and generous but will tell you when you are off track, the writing isn't any good, or I'm full of myself. She is good at everything, but her humility doesn't let her see it. She is insightful and sees when people are hurting. She is a saint, a friend, a hero. She is a disciple of Christ—always serving, always giving, always loving.

I am eternally grateful to my teachers in the gospel. Elizabeth Keeler, Mel Heaps, and Paul Duncan made the scriptures come alive in early-morning seminary. From encouraging me to *actually* read them to taping life-sized Goliath cutouts to the wall, they introduced me to the Savior by their dedication and faith. Their enthusiasm for the gospel and insights into scripture make them my teachers and my first teacher-heroes. I am in your debt, dear teachers.

I have many scholarly mentors. Alonzo L. Gaskill is one of the best. His books on symbolism set me on the path of loving scripture. I will never forget picking up one of his books while waiting for a business appointment in Northern California. It was like I was reading scripture for the first time. The insights, the joy, the pure love of Christ flowed from the pages. I devoured every word. I reread the scriptures, and the "scales fell from my eyes." I became a fan. Then, he became my friend and mentor. More than just ancient languages and history, I learned that scholarship is more than just study but about faith. Discipleship is about loving God and your neighbor. Alonzo embodies the gospel of Jesus Christ, and it is reflected in his scholarship. He loves Christ, and it shows in his every word and deed.

I have great cheerleaders, friends like Coralie Harless, who continually encourage me. She is the friend who sends texts and voicemails praising and encouraging my every work. She makes me feel like a giant, a success at every turn. Everyone needs a Coralie in their life.

I am grateful for Cohort F. at Gonzaga's Master of Theology and Leadership program. Delilah, Julie, Kathryn, Maureen, Will, Linda, Ann, CeCe, Steven, Chuck, Blaise, Nathan, Lauren, Francis, Anita, Jai, and Cubby (and the professors), I have learned that God can teach us all in many ways. Gonzaga has indeed shown me that everything we know, everything we do, and everyone we meet can lead to God. Indeed, all things teach of Him.

This humble work could not be done without each of them. They are my friends. They are my heroes.

Ad Majorem Dei Gloriam—For the Greater Glory of God!

FIRST THINGS

We all fail. That seems to be our common lot in life. We make mistakes. At times we don't understand. Or we rebel purposefully. We also have physical challenges, mental health hurdles, and the woes of a fallen world.

Despite all of that, there is good news. It is a message we have probably all heard but sometimes forget, or don't believe is for us. The good news is that Jesus has come! He has overcome this world—the hurts, the failings, even death. With Him, we will never fail.

And that is good news. With God, we will prevail.

This book is about real people like you and me. The Old Testament is full of their stories of when they found God. In the stories of their lives, we see real people with highs and lows. They have moments of faith. They show times when they are heroic and fantastic, obey the Lord, and see miracles happen. Their stories also tell of their failings. They have moments of doubt, make mistakes, and at times misunderstand.

God chooses people from all walks of life. They can be kings and prophets or shepherds and musicians. All of them make mistakes. At times, they can be the less fortunate, the marginalized, or the outcast. They are afraid, wrong, or sinful.

Scripture is great because it shares the stories of people when they are real. They are heroes despite their failings. They make mistakes, and God uses them anyway. The end of Genesis says it perfectly. After Joseph receives his coat of many colors, his brothers sell him into slavery, and he overcomes it to save them from famine. He tells his brothers,

"Even though you intended to do me harm, God intended it for good, in order to preserve a numerous people as he is doing today" (NRSV, Genesis 50:20). Despite our mistakes and our failings, God will preserve us as we turn to Him. We can become instruments in His hand.

These are the real heroes of the Old Testament.

The heroes are the people who fail, struggle, and are imperfect, and yet have the strength to return to God. The scriptures say it best. Let's hear a few more thoughts on it directly from them.

"And forgive Your people who have sinned against You and all their transgressions which they have transgressed against You, and make them objects of compassion before those who have taken them captive, that they may have compassion on them" (NRSV, 1 Kings 8:50).

"For You, Lord, are good, and ready to forgive, And abundant in lovingkindness to all who call upon You" (NRSV, Psalm 86:5).

By following our Father and becoming a disciple of Jesus Christ, we can become heroes in our own lives. The good news is that through the Atonement of Jesus Christ, we can overcome. As the modern house of Israel, we can tap into that power. Let God prevail.[1]

READING SCRIPTURE

Scripture is dynamic. It is a way for God to tell the story of how He worked in the past and how He works today. Much of scripture is a story, a narrative. Those stories resonate with us across time and culture because they are stories. The prophets told stories rather than giving a checklist of instructions (granted, there are a few sections like that in scripture). Jesus taught in parables. The Book of Mormon recounts the rise and failure of an entire people. Starting

---

1 A note on scriptural interpretation. Growing up, I thought that scriptures had "a" singular interpretation. My job was to find out what it was. Or I could "cheat" and find a conference talk and see what a prophet or apostle said it meant. It wasn't a terrible idea. It had some merit. If a General Authority told me what it meant, I could feel confident that it was correct. That is still correct today. However, I didn't understand how scripture works.

with one family, we learn how they came to understand the Savior and His plan of salvation. The Old Testament is composed of great quantities of narratives. The power of stories is that their interpretation is fluid. The Spirit can use those stories to touch our hearts where we are—with what we need. Most scripture stories don't end with a moral at the end, with everything neatly tied up in a bow. They invite us to ponder, pray, and experiment upon the word (see Alma 32). Rather than a tidy conclusion, scriptures invite us to see ourselves in the lives of others. We ponder, wrestle, and consider what it all means. We don't nibble. We feast.

Scripture Cheat Sheet

There are two keys to the power of scripture stories. Stories can make us *feel*. The first key to unlocking these feelings is understanding their world. If we understand their circumstances, the time, and the culture in which they lived, we know them. We care about the people and what is happening in their lives. We may cheer for them and root for their victory. We may also fear the tyranny around them, afraid for the enemies that are on the rise. Their mistakes and sins make us cringe and worry, even feel anxiety for them. Biblical stories are about more than sharing data, history, and background. That first key is context. Context helps us feel what they were feeling, see what they saw, and live like they lived. Insights into the culture, history, language, and people can help us know what the events meant to those people, in their time, within their unique culture. The people of the Old Testament lived in a time unlike ours. How they lived, what they ate and wore, and how they treated each other was different from the twenty-first century. The events gain power and impact when we understand what was happening and what it meant to them.

The second key to scripture stories is how they affect us. They are about inviting us to respond, interact, and interpret what is going on. Scriptures aren't just a history or a clever tale. They are invitations. They urge us to see ourselves in the stories, people, and events. The impact, the power, is where *we let these stories in.* These stories can affect us. They can change us *if we let them.* Our responses help us make sense of the story. By allowing the characters—their hopes, dreams, fears, and mistakes—into our hearts, we draw the power of the scriptures into our own story. This key unlocks the power of the Savior in our lives. When we listen for the gospel of Jesus Christ in the pages, when we let Him change us, these stories become potent and real. In each page we can see the Lord as He guides, directs, and teaches us. We will hear Him.

In this book, we will try to do both. We will take a little time to try and understand the history, context, and language of the ancients to understand what they did and feel what they felt. More important, we are invited into the story. I invite you to jump in, see yourselves in these stories, and liken them to your own life. There is no one interpretation of a story—there is only what you see and what the Spirit invites you to see there. So, jump on in, try it on, and let the stories become your friends and family. Let these stories become your story.

A simple tool that will help us use these two keys is a clear translation. I will also use a translation that is a little easier to read for modern readers, the New Revised Standard Version (NRSV), or in some cases, my translation. I love the King James Version (KJV); it is the translation I grew up with. Its language is poetic, but it can be a little old-fashioned and requires clarifying. So, I'll just skip that part and use a translation that is more like our modern English. You can open your scriptures, turn on an app, and read the KJV and NRSV, and many other translations, side by side. I invite you to give it a try. It can really help explain the language and story. If I am ever unclear, look it up. "When in doubt, check it out." Don't let me be the expert, but let the scriptures speak to you in the way with which you're most comfortable.

Scripture is some of the strongest commentaries on itself. The New Testament comments and explores the Old Testament. The Book of Mormon prophets constantly look back to Old Testament prophets and stories and see their own lives reflected in it. Abraham and Moses both share insights in the Pearl of Great Price we do not have any other place. The Doctrine and Covenants and modern prophets have all discussed other scripture, its meaning, and its implication. This book takes the stories as they are. We may peek into other scripture, but for the most part we'll stick to the stories in their own place.

I'm going to give some interpretation and application. If you don't like my take, that's okay. I will probably change my mind occasionally as I learn new things. And that, my friend, is part of their power. The scriptures, not an interpretation (including this modest book), are the power. The scriptures, and their ability to invite the Holy Spirit, are the real key. Hopefully, this book will invite you to turn to the Book itself, to ask the Spirit into your life to give you meaning and insights. It is perfectly normal to ask a question, write notes to yourself, and stump your Sunday School teacher. I believe doctrines of The Church of Jesus Christ of Latter-day Saints are perfect, and scriptures hold eternal truths. I also believe we are to apply them. Thus, scripture application isn't always about "the" answer. It is about an answer you need right now. That's how it is supposed to work. So, jump on in, and find out what these stories of the Old Testament are all about.

There is one more bonus key to understanding scripture. We can turn to the Lord and ask for the Holy Spirit. Book of Mormon prophet Nephi encouraged us to turn to the Spirit of the Lord for insights. When scripture gets tricky or unclear, we can remember's Nephi words: "The mysteries of God . . . unfolded unto them, by the power of the Holy Ghost" (1 Nephi 10:19). Elder Bruce R. McConkie of the Quorum of the Twelve said, "Each pronouncement in the holy scriptures . . . is so written as to reveal little or much, depending on the spiritual capacity of the student."[2]

2. Bruce R. McConkie, *A New Witness for the Articles of Faith* (Salt Lake City: Deseret Book Co., 1985), 71.

THE FAMILY OF ABRAHAM

Abraham and Isaac

ABRAHAM COMMANDED
TO SACRIFICE HIS ONLY SON

Readers of the Bible will remember the tense and heart-wrenching scene in Genesis 22 when God tests Abraham and asks him to sacrifice his promised and beloved son. Abraham had received a covenant from God that he would be blessed and, in turn, bless all people, all nations. God told Abraham he would have the priesthood, God's authority; a promised land; and a posterity as numerous as the stars in the heavens and the sands on the seashore.

And then "God did test Abraham" (Genesis 22:1). Abraham immediately responds, "Here I am!"

God tells Abraham to take his only son, Isaac, to a mountain called Moriah and offer him as a burnt offering sacrifice. Abraham responds to this drastic and overwhelming command by planning to do it. He gets up early in the morning, responding to God's command at the earliest moment. He prepares some supplies and takes Isaac and a few servants. Abraham even chops the wood they will need for the offering, and they head out to Moriah.

For three days they travel, and Abraham sees the site up ahead. He instructs the servants to stay behind, telling them, "Stay here with the donkey; the boy and I will go over there; we will worship, and then we will come back to you." Then, they arrive at the spot. Abraham gives the wood to Isaac to carry, he takes the fire (presumably a torch) and the knife, and they continue on together. During the final walk, Isaac calls out to Abraham, "Father!" Once again, Abraham responds, "Here I am," and lovingly adds, "my son."

Isaac asks, "The fire and the wood are here, but where is the lamb for a burnt offering?"

Abraham responds, "God himself will provide the lamb for a burnt offering, my son" (NRSV, Genesis 22:8). With that pronouncement, the two walk on together.

When Abraham reaches the spot that God had showed him, he builds an altar and lays the wood in order. He then binds Isaac on top of the altar. Abraham raises his hand with the knife upraised to kill Isaac.

But, right then, at that very moment, the Lord calls to Abraham, "Abraham, Abraham!"

And for the third time, Abraham answers, "Here I am!"

"Do not lay your hand on the boy or do anything to him; for now, I know that you fear God since you have not withheld your son, your only son, from me" (NRSV, Genesis 22:12).

And there, stuck by his horns in a thicket, is a male lamb, a ram. Abraham offers it as a sacrifice instead of his son. And the place is named "The Lord will provide." Then, the angel of the Lord calls out to Abraham again and tells him, "Because you have done this, and you have not withheld your son, your only son, I will indeed bless you, and I will make your offspring as numerous as the stars of heaven and as the sand that is on the seashore. And your offspring shall possess the gate of their enemies, and by your offspring shall all the earth gain blessing for themselves, because you have obeyed my voice" (NRSV, Genesis 22:16–18).

A STORY THAT ASKS US TO PAUSE

This story is one of the most dramatic and shocking in all of scripture. It is also one of the most interpreted, studied, and questioned.[1] In twenty short verses, many perplexing questions are set before us. The event causes us to question what is going on, its motives, and God's purpose in asking this of Abraham. It is easy to do one of two things: read through it quickly, not asking ourselves the tough questions, or skip it altogether as a story we already know. Perhaps the uncomfortable, and at times the unanswerable, questions of this disturbing story are more easily left unexamined. But those moments of tension and unease, the questions that the story prompts, are the *power behind this story.* Yes, it is a story with heroes, but it also leaves us with as many questions as answers. Why would God ask Abraham to do such a thing? Why would Abraham do it? Did Abraham know it was a test? Is this just an analogy?

It is a scriptural account that tells us very little about the characters and the people we are learning from and emulating. Unlike scriptures that have a lot of detail and explain its reason, this story is unexpressed. Because there is so little about the story's motives and the characters' feelings, we are left in the dark, out of balance and with uncertainty. A brief story about a biblical patriarch being asked to enact human sacrifice *should* make us uncomfortable. A story like this *should* make us pause and consider, ask questions, and create uncertainty. Rather than rush over the story, or skip it altogether, this story asks us to stop, think, and examine it. This story invites us to pause.

But we're jumping ahead. Let's take that pause and tackle this incredible story of faith and sacrifice, uncertainty, and tension, one step at a time. This is the story of the Binding of Isaac.

THE BINDING OF ISAAC

It is one of the most common and perplexing stories in history. It is a story that's been interpreted for millennia, and yet it still requires more interpretation, more thought, and more prayer.

---

1. Christine Hayes, *Introduction to the Bible* (New Haven: Yale University Press, 2012), 85.

This story is called the Binding of Isaac, or the *Akedah* in Hebrew. *Akedah* means binding, and as Isaac survived, we call it the Binding of Isaac.[2] There are three main characters in this story: Abraham, Isaac, and God. We'll examine each one.

What Has Gone on Before

You know how some TV series recap everything that has happened at the beginning of each episode? If you took a break or forgot all the details, the program kindly reviews all the essential points so that you can jump back into the story. That's what we need to do here, starting with the Creation (if you remember this part, you can skip on ahead to the story of Isaac. It is a great story, though, so you may want to reread it anyway).

But Isaac's story starts before. He is part of Abraham and Sarah's story.

Laying the Groundwork

This is the first family, as it were, the family God chooses to start His covenant. The story of everything in the book of Genesis begins with humanity placed in a garden. They are perfect, and they are God's culminating creation. Man and woman, together, are His image-bearers. In the middle of the garden is two trees—the tree of the knowledge of good and evil and the tree of life. God gives humanity a choice, and we choose knowledge. Out of the garden, we learn for ourselves how to choose and see if we'll follow the Lord.[3]

How does humanity do? Well, it starts with Cain and Abel, so, frankly, that's a bit of a disastrous way to start. If fratricide doesn't show what a terrible job we do on our own, then I suppose we won't get the hint. It doesn't look too good, choosing for ourselves. Then it goes from bad to worse. In fact, in the first few chapters, humanity

---

2. Nahum M. Sarna, *Understanding Genesis* (New York: The Jewish Theological Seminary), 160.
3. Genesis 1–4

has become so corrupt and evil that God wipes out most people in a flood, saving just eight on an ark, captained by a prophet named Noah. Even with an earthly reset, it isn't long until things turn evil again. People choose to follow their hearts and not the Lord. This story would seem like a tragedy, but God still has a plan that will save His children. It is at this point of the story that God chooses a family.

The Family of Abraham and the Covenant

While it looks like humanity is doomed, history takes a turn. God hasn't given up on His family at all. He has a plan to teach us how to live and provides a Savior to lead us back to His presence. Remarkably, this plan of salvation begins most surprisingly. Rather than start with something powerful and mighty like a king or queen, a sign from the heavens, or a natural disaster, God starts with a family—the family of Abraham.

Choosing a Family

How does God go about saving the world? He finds the least likely of fellows. God calls Abraham,[4] and Abraham goes. He has no support from his family, no children of his own, no people, no town, no country. It is as if God is choosing to start from the ground up. Abraham is bare-bones, rock bottom, landless, and wandering. In choosing Abraham, God shows us that Abraham is mighty because God is mighty. Alone, Abraham is not very formidable. He isn't a king or powerful by himself. He is childless, without a home, without a people.

It is then that God makes a promise, a covenant. He promises Abraham that he will have the priesthood, a promised land, prosperity, and a family.[5] Through him, all people, all nations, all

---

4. I will refer to Abraham throughout the Genesis story regardless of timing of his name change. While he is Abram and becomes Abraham later, it is distracts from the story. For clarity, I will refer to him as Abraham.
5. Genesis 12, 15, 17; Abraham 2:9–11, 3:14

11

time will be blessed when they obey the laws and ordinances of the gospel.[6] Through the family and covenant of Abraham, the gospel of the Lord will be shared throughout the world. The gospel of Jesus Christ, and promises of eternal life, are given to all.

A crucial element of this great saving part of the covenant is that Abraham will have a family. It is through Abraham's family that God shares the gospel of salvation. And that's where Isaac comes in. Now, it might seem like all this history and backstory is a friendly reminder. But it is far more. It is vitally important to understanding the story of the Binding of Isaac. Isaac is the promised son, from the promised family, who will give everyone blessings and lead them to eternal life.

The Binding of Isaac is additionally mind-boggling because Isaac is part of this promise of salvation. Through Abraham and Isaac, the promised son, all of humanity—every man, woman, and child, past present, and future—will have the salvation of Jesus Christ. So, when we tell the story of Isaac, we remember all that background. We recall the innumerable bad times, the despair, the failings of the human family. And we are excited and thrilled that God has a Savior planned who will be one of the blessings of this covenant through the family of Abraham, through the promised son, Isaac. If Isaac dies, how will all that promise be fulfilled?

But first, let's talk about Abraham.

ABRAHAM

We have already touched on Abraham's history as God continues His plan for salvation. But what of that man? As we read the story of the Binding of Isaac, we can't help but ask ourselves why Abraham, who loved his son, this promised miracle child, would even consider such an act. That's when we return to what we know about Abraham.

---

6. Galatians 3:26–29, 4:1–7; Doctrine and Covenants 84:33–40

Abraham is one of the patriarchs, the founding fathers of scriptures, and while there are many stories of him, we will touch on just a few. Each of those stories tells us about him, his background, and his motivations. Before we get to the Binding of Isaac, we engage in a series of stories about Abraham. These narratives give us knowledge and foundations about God and Abraham on which we can build. These glimpses into the heart of Abraham invite us to ask questions, wrestle, and ponder his character. We're expected to remember these stories and place the binding in its proper context so that the near-sacrifice of Isaac tells us not only of Isaac but of Abraham and his relationship to God. They also should prompt us to reflect on our own motivations. As we peer into Abraham's heart, we uncover our own.

Beginnings

Abraham's story starts implausibly. He is called to leave—drop what he's doing, pack up, and leave. He's told to leave his ancestral home and family because God asks him to. And just like that, with no pause, no hesitation, he obeys. Genesis 12 says, "Now the Lord said to Abram, 'Go from your country and your kindred and your father's house to the land that I will show you' . . . So Abram went" (NRSV, Genesis 12:1, 4).

We know very little of Abraham. In our opening verses, our introduction to him is that he does what God asks without hesitation. God says to leave, and Abraham leaves. It doesn't even say he tells his wife or family. He makes no plans. He packs nothing first. Immediately, and without question, he does what he's asked.

Of course, Abraham probably did pack and tell his family. A person doesn't take their wife and nephew and leave their home without plans or packing. Indeed, we learn in the following few verses that he does that. But the way it is written that he leaves and *then* packs, while logistically improbable, is intended to tell us about Abraham. By placing God's command *immediately* followed by Abraham's instant obedience, the scriptural author wants to point out that Abraham was *immediately* obedient to divine commands. God asks, and there is no stopping, no asking, no packing—just obedience. It is this utter devotion to God that sets Abraham apart from others. Remembering the failings of the human family until now, at least how the story of Genesis lays it out, we see that unyielding obedience to God distinguishes Abraham from all those who have come before.

One thing we know about Abraham is that he is unfailingly obedient.

Abraham Loves His Sons

Early in the story, Abraham is childless. He has no one to carry on his name and fulfill the promise of the Lord. Then, he has a son by Hagar, Sarah's maid. Ishmael is the long-awaited child. His name means "God hears" (Genesis 16:11).[7] Indeed, God heard Abraham's desire for a child and blessed him with Ishmael. Yet, just before the binding, we hear of Abraham pushing Ishmael out.

Sarah is barren. Perhaps to help fulfill God's covenant promise, and in an ancient tradition, she gives up Hagar, her handmaiden, to serve as a way to have a child.[8] Hagar's son, Ishmael, looks like the son that will carry on the Abrahamic covenant. Then, miraculously, Sarah conceives and gives birth to Isaac. We retell that story a little later. For now, it is enough to remember it in brief.

Ishmael and Isaac

Infant mortality rates were very high. Having a child live past infancy was a cause for celebration. Once Isaac was old enough to eat solid food and leave his mother, it indicated that he survived and passed an impressive milestone. In addition to survival, Isaac's weaning also meant that Isaac would receive the birthright, and Ishmael,

---

7. Alonzo L. Gaskill, *The Lost Language of Symbolism* (Salt Lake City: Deseret Book, 2003), 220..
8. Hayes, *Introduction to the Bible*, 80.

the older son, would not. That is when the much older Ishmael teases and threatens little Isaac. The word used for teasing means more than just playing or lightly mocking. We see the same word when the Philistines release Samson after blinding him, imprisoning him, and bringing him out "to play," tying him to a pillar (see Judges 16:25). Ishmael's play with Isaac is more than a gentle ribbing between siblings and is very alarming (see Genesis 21:6).

Ishmael is also thirteen or fourteen years older than Isaac.[9] Isaac is only a toddler, say two or three years old, so Ishmael would be closer to sixteen or seventeen. Ishmael is a young man compared to a vulnerable toddler. When Sarah learns of Ishmael's actions, she is exceedingly worried for Isaac's safety. She asks Abraham to drive out Hagar and Ishmael, as is her right (see Genesis 17:15–25).

In this story, Abraham is pushing out Ishmael, the only beloved son of Hagar. We know from Genesis 17 that Abraham loved Ishmael dearly. For when the Lord promises Abraham a family, as one of the blessings of the covenant, Abraham says, "Oh that Ishmael might live in your sight!" (NRSV, Genesis 17:18). God promises Ishmael blessings but tells Abraham that Isaac, Sarah's son, will fulfill and carry on the covenant promises. Abraham loves his son Ishmael deeply. Is God testing Abraham? What is Abraham being taught? Is this a trial? A punishment? A test?

What Does It Mean?

The Bible doesn't tell us what it means. And that may just be the point.

The interpretation of this story—why Ishmael was not chosen, why he was cast out even though Abraham loved him—is not clear. Indeed, perhaps that is the point. We have a few clues to help us understand the family and social dynamics of over 3,000 years ago.

The scarcity of the narrative builds tension, draws us in, and invites us to ask questions. The lack of details heightens the

---

9. Ibid., 83.

emotions of the event. Erich Auerbach, in his groundbreaking work on biblical narrative says,

> The decisive points of the narrative alone are emphasized. . . . Time and place are undefined and call for interpretation; thoughts and feelings remain unexpressed, are only suggested by the silence and the fragmentary speeches; the whole permeated with the most unrelieved suspense and directed toward a single goal . . . remains a mysterious and fraught with background.[10]

In contrast, think of a story told in excruciating detail—anything by Charles Dickens or even a Harry Potter novel. In those narratives, we are told what the characters are thinking, what they are feeling, and every tiny detail. In those stories, we are told what happens, why it happens, and what drives the characters to do what they do. There is no mystery there. While that is helpful and highly entertaining, it is not scripture. Keeping the details ambiguous creates tension. I love how Auerbach describes it: "Fraught with background."[11]

The scriptural narrative *invites us* to search for answers. We look for connections in how the Lord works with others. We delve into the eternal mysteries and search for "treasures of knowledge" (D&C 89:19). By creating tension and inviting questions, we are invited into the story. We must answer the questions for ourselves.

Abraham's Character

Another story tells us important details about Abraham's heart. It's one we gloss over, but it's the story of Sodom and Gomorrah in Genesis 18 and 19. As part of Abraham's character development,

---

10. Erich Auerbach, *Mimesis: The Representation of Reality in Western Literature,* trans. Willard R. Trask (Princeton, NJ: Princeton University Press, 1968), 11–12.
11. Ibid.,, 12.

he's placed in the impossible position of saving horrible people. In this story we catch a glimpse into Abraham's character, motivations, and desires.

Sodom and Gomorrah is full of terrible wickedness. There are multiple cities, called "the cities on the plain," and they are wealthy, powerful, and growing as a group. Yet, they are inhospitable (see Genesis 18:21). One of the desert's highest and most essential laws is to extend hospitality to strangers (see Leviticus 19:34). Sadly, the people of the city had tried to abuse several angelic visitors. In showing this insight, we get a peek into the morals of the city of Sodom and Gomorrah. We learn that the whole city is going to be destroyed. And here's where the story of Abraham comes back into play in Genesis 18 and 19. We hear that Abraham argues with God.

Notice how we come to these conclusions about the morality of the people and the heart of Abraham. The scriptural author shows us, *by their actions* rather than a conclusion, that they were corrupt and terrible. The scripture could have just said, "The people were terrible. You wouldn't like them. I'm serious, and there wasn't one innocent person in the whole city." But we aren't told that. We experience it. When we share the experience, when we place ourselves into the story, living what they lived, we can learn what they learned.

LEARNING ABOUT GOD'S CHARACTER

Upon learning of the destruction of the cities, Abraham asks God, "Will you sweep the innocent along with the guilty" (NRSV, Genesis 18:23)? It's a rhetorical question. He's asking whether God would do such injustice if there were innocent people in the city. Would God wipe them out? It's for us to answer the question, how can a just God act so and unjustly? This question is setting us up for the binding. We remember God is just, and so we put that little nugget of truth, that treasure, in the back of our minds. In just a few chapters, we have to recall it to understand the nature of Abraham and the heart of God.

We have to ask ourselves, does God punish the wicked? Does association punish the innocent? Does the wickedness of the majority overrule the others? Does God wipe them all out and "settle up on the other side"? How is this supposed to work exactly? It is at this moment, with this negotiation, that we learn something about both Abraham and God.

Abraham starts to haggle with the Lord. Abraham is banking on the fact that God is merciful. He asks, "Well, what if there were fifty innocent people?"

The Lord says, "Fine, if there are fifty innocent people, I will not destroy."

I love this part. Abraham pushes the issue. "Well, what if there are forty-five innocent people? Would you still destroy the city?"

And God says, "No, I'll give it to you. If there are forty-five, I won't."

They keep going down, and eventually Abraham whittles the number down to ten. We should be thinking, "Wow, ten people. For ten innocent people, the Lord will not destroy Sodom." This is a very terrible city.

Ten innocent people are not found. They are guilty, the scripture says, to the last man (see Genesis 19:25). There are no innocent people. Thus, Sodom and the other four cities of the plain are destroyed, wiped out. Lot, Abraham's nephew, lives in one of these cities and is saved because of God's love for Abraham. Genesis 19:29 says, "God remembered Abraham, and sent Lot out of the midst of the upheaval."

What does this tell us about Abraham?

Abraham cares. He cares about people. He is willing to negotiate, haggle, do whatever he can to save the people. The haggling story might be a bit weird, but that's not the point I'm trying to make here. The point is that Abraham cares about people. He cares even about people he does not know. He cares about the innocent. He cares about the whole city—about all of them. Lot isn't a big prize, but Abraham loves him, too. The people of Sodom and cities of the plain aren't worthy, but Abraham is willing to love them. Abraham is willing to fight for them.

DIALOGUE IN THE BIBLE

Rarely do we find dialogue in the Bible. Most stories are told very briefly with little "back and forth." When it does happen, it is significant, and we should pay attention.[12]

Why does God let Abraham negotiate? What does Abraham have to learn about himself? In allowing Abraham to discuss, he learns that he cares. He learns that he is willing to fight for people he does not even know. God already knew it. Now, Abraham does. It is also important for us to know, to better understand the Binding of Isaac.

Where does that leave us? How do we get a story, then? How do we reconcile this? Abraham was willing to push out his son, Hagar's only beloved son. Yet, the same man would defend the unrighteous and nameless population of Sodom. Abraham is willing to be sacrificed. He says, "Let me take it upon myself . . . I who am but dust and ashes" (Genesis 18:27). After those stories, it is *then* we are introduced to Abraham and the Binding of Isaac.

That brings us back around full circle to Abraham and the Binding of Isaac. So, what does this tell us about Abraham?

A STORY OF CONTRADICTIONS

In Abraham, we have a story of contradictions. We have a man who seemingly casts out his son Ishmael, whom he loves. We learn that Abraham is complex. Like us, he is faithful but also is pulled in other directions. By sharing both stories of Abraham, we are invited into the complexity of his life. Abraham's willingness to

---

12. Robert Alter, *The Art of Biblical Narrative* (New York: Basic Books, 2011), 24, 42, 68.

fight for others is contrasted with him sending away his beloved older son. We are left with a story of a complex man who wants and knows how to do the right thing but may not always do so. Sound familiar? By showing us the two contrasting sides of Abraham, we enter the story of the Binding of Isaac, unsure what Abraham will do. Will he be the faithful one who immediately responds to the Lord's commands? Or will he bargain and question, begging for Isaac's life? Will Abraham fight for Isaac, like he did the people of Sodom?

Which Abraham are we meeting when we get to the Binding of Isaac?

The stories do not always have answers. What they do have are real people struggling to make decisions. Their successes and failures are there for us to see. There is no careful editing, only telling us of their brilliant accomplishments. The scriptures show us real people with successes on one page and utter failings on the next. In these "real" people, these heroes, we see ourselves. We must use wisdom to understand how to apply the contradictions, challenges, and real-life experiences to our own life. If God is willing to work with them, it means He is also willing to work with us.

It's time to meet our next character in the story, Isaac.

ISAAC

In the Binding of Isaac, we meet a character who says only a dozen words in the story. He has scarcely been introduced to us before, except that he is the promised miracle child. Isaac's name means "he laughs."[13] The name echoes the joy of his parents, the miracle of his birth, the chosen child who is finally here. And to two elderly parents, is it any wonder that Abraham and Sarah laugh? So, if the joy of a child, a long-awaited miracle child, is what we first think of Isaac, we cannot forget Isaac's "other" story

---

13. Hayes, *Introduction to the Bible*, 82.

in which his father takes him to a hillside to sacrifice him. The story of Isaac is a story of both faith and fear, promise and sacrifice, laughter and desperation.

Names

Biblical narrative does not give us much background. We learn about the characters and people through their actions. We also learn about them through the meaning of their names. Anciently names indicated some vital character or attribute of the bearer. It could be something the parents saw in the baby, or perhaps, it was a result of God's connection to their lives. The name could also be aspirational—something we hope is true about the person. Alonzo Gaskill wrote, "In ancient scripture, names were generally given in order to indicate something about the nature, character, experience, or function of the person, place or nation named."[14] Isaac, "he laughs," is a child of surprise, joy, and relief. He is a promise fulfilled.

THE ABRAHAMIC COVENANT

We remember the promises of the Lord's covenant: priesthood, promised land, posterity, and prosperity. Following the story of Genesis, we have anxiously awaited God's promised family through Abraham and Sarah. We wondered if it was going to be Ishmael who would fulfill God's promises. Later, we learned it was Isaac. Isaac has little backstory besides this. Yes, Ishmael did threaten him and was driven out from the family, but other than that, Isaac's story so far is quiet.

"Invisible" is how Isaac is characterized. He is the least visible of the patriarchs and matriarchs.[15] While all the other families have journeys to or from the promised land, Isaac is stationary. He never

---

14. Alonzo L. Gaskill, *The Lost Language of Symbolism* (Salt Lake City: Deseret Book Company, 2003), location 6311.
15. Ibid.,, 80.

leaves Canaan. He is somehow attached to the land, and his story reflects that static state. Abraham and Sarah come from Ur, go to Egypt, and return. Rebekah is found outside with extended family and brought into the promised land. Jacob has a very dynamic story, fleeing and then returning a changed man. And later, Jacob's family, through Joseph of Egypt, leave for Egypt to escape a famine. All of them journey, change and grow, are tested, and move in and out of the promised land. Everyone, that is, except Isaac. Isaac's test and life are in one place. He is to obey the covenant, and struggle with his own family. He is connected to the promised land. As the promised son, his life echoes the challenges of Canaan. Isaac is the promised land, and so, he never leaves.

Isaac, the promised child, is one of the most invisible of all the ancient ancestors. He's the most passive of the patriarchs. Indeed, if we look at the story of his wife, Rebekah, we see that she's one of the most active. They're almost like a point-counterpoint—a set of opposites that draw our attention to both. As married partners, it is helpful to look at them together.

REBEKAH

Rebekah is a woman of action. Her life deserves more detail than just this overview. But for now, let's review how she is contrasted to her husband, Isaac.

We haven't met her at the time of the binding, but her life is a good contrast to Isaac's. She gives us insights into this quiet patriarch, even though they haven't met yet.

Her story begins in Genesis 24 when Abraham's servant, Eliezar, is sent to find a suitable partner for Isaac. That should be our first clue that there is no one local that is a good match. Isaac has no equal, no partner, no one to match his faith. He needs an equal partner in the Lord. That's when we meet Rebekah.

Eliezar travels back to the family of Terah, Abraham's father. He is a special envoy entrusted to find Isaac's covenant partner. When he arrives in the area where he hopes to find her, he prays, "O Lord,

God of my master Abraham, please grant me success today and show steadfast love to my master Abraham" (Genesis 24:12) Eliezar invokes the covenant. By saying "steadfast love," he is reminding the Lord of his promises. Steadfast love is covenantal love, faith in keeping your promise. This phrase is repeated over and over in scriptures, like a hyperlink to remind us of the covenant. In the New Testament the phrase is "grace and truth." Calling on the Lord to remember His servants, and always faithful to His promises, we have hope. We know that his prayer will be answered with a woman equal to our hero. That woman is Rebekah.

She enters the story. Her actions are quick and decisive:

- She quickly offers hospitality to strangers.
- She quickly waters their camels.
- She quickly obeys.
- She quickly commits to marriage.
- She immediately, upon arriving, is married. She waits for no one.
- She quickly engages Isaac to have a family.

Rebekah is a woman of action. When God requires it, Rebekah does not hesitate to act. When she learns Jacob, the younger twin, will receive the birthright, she jumps in to ensure it happens.

Where Isaac is patient, Rebekah moves. She is the first to obey, the first to act. She is like an ancient Peter, always jumping in 100 percent. I have a feeling if Rebekah had been in the boat on the Sea of Galilee when the Lord called, she and Peter would have been pushing each other back to see who could jump out of the boat first.

By contrast, Isaac avoids confrontation. When Isaac and Rebekah's worldly wealth grows and their household flourishes, the nearby Philistines, led by a man named Abimelek, complain they are too powerful. Isaac, powerful? We don't think of him as being powerful because of his quiet nature. But here it is. Genesis 26:17 says that Isaac is very blessed and exceedingly powerful. What does Isaac do—this wealthy man who has a huge household, men at his command, and the Lord on his side? He moves. He avoids the confrontation. He moves to a new part of the promised land, rebuilds the wells so desperately needed to survive, and thrives there.

The portrait of Isaac is a man of great faith. A powerful man yet controlled, a perfect example of meekness. He is a man of great and abiding love and faith. He is the promised child, the heir to God's promise of salvation to Abraham and all the world. He is meek and mighty, yet disciplined. He is faithful, acting, and obeying. He is, like his name, joy at receiving a long-expected blessing.

GOD

The final character in this story is the Lord. While we focus on understanding the motivations that drive Abraham and, in some part, Isaac, ever-present is the Lord.

In scripture, we do not always get all the "whys." Instead, we are forced to contemplate. In the absence of clear answers, we have to ask questions. In the story of Abraham and Isaac, we are not given answers. We aren't given very much at all. In just a few short verses, we must sit with questions, roll them over in our minds, and figure them out. If, that is, we allow ourselves to delve into the story. Prompting only questions, inviting us to reflect on our own lives, is one of the great powers of scripture. By pondering its depths, asking God for the Holy Spirit to guide and teach us, He can show us meanings and insights, not just in the lives of ancient people but in our own.

The story makes us ask questions like this:

- Why did God test Abraham?
- Did Abraham know it was a test? Do we know when we are being tested?
- What about Isaac? Did he understand what was happening? Could he have gotten away?
- What was Abraham thinking while they walked for three days? And Isaac? What was going through his head during the long walk?

- Who are these servants? Did they understand what was happening? We know nothing about them. Who are they? What is their role?
- What about Sarah? Where is she in this story? What will happen to her only son?
- What of the covenant? Will God bless Abraham, and all the nations, if Isaac dies? How will God keep His promises when things seem impossible?

This is not just a story of God and Abraham and Isaac. It is a story of God and us—you and me.

Now, we are ready to return to the story of Abraham, Isaac, and the Lord. Now that we have firmly in our minds the paradox that is Abraham, the quiet faith that is Isaac, and the complexity of God, we are ready to enter the story of the Binding of Isaac.

THE BINDING OF ISAAC, GENESIS 22

"After these things, God tested Abraham" (NRSV, Genesis 22:1).

The story starts suddenly and abruptly. After all the blessings Abraham has received in his life, a turning point has arrived. We are jolted into the story, off-kilter and already tense. We are shocked into the story, like the emotions the story evokes. We will be spiritually jolted like this introduction.

"[God] said unto him, 'Abraham!' And he said, 'Here I am'" (NRSV, Genesis 22:1).

The Lord calls Abraham. And like so many other examples, from the Savior to Moses responding to the call to serve the Father, it is a response unlike any other.

Hineni. It means "Here I am." In Hebrew *hen* means "behold," and *ani* means "me."[16] From there, we get the idea of "Behold!" or "Here I am." Sometimes, you'll see translations say either "here

---

16. F. Brown, S. Driver, and C. Briggs, *The Brown-Driver-Briggs Hebrew and English Lexicon* (Boston: Hendrickson Publishers, 2004), 243.

I am" or "behold." Embedded in the phrase is more than just acknowledging we are in a place. It means we are ready to obey. The term means we are willing to act.

Hineni is used at a critical turning point in someone's life, like Moses being called from the burning bush. "Here I am!" (Exodus 3:4) He is saying he's ready to do whatever the Lord commands. Later we meet the young prophet Samuel. When he doesn't recognize the Lord's voice, he goes to the priest Eli, who explains to him how to respond to a call from the Lord (see 1 Samuel 3:4–8). When Isaiah answers the Lord's question, "Whom shall I send?" Isaiah responds, "*Hineni*. Here I am. Send me" (Isaiah 6:8). In the Great Council, when the Father explained His grand plan of salvation and asked who the Savior would be, our Lord stood up and said, "*Hineni*. Here I am. Send me" (Abraham 3:24–27).

When the Lord calls, we respond ready for action, prepared to change, prepared to follow. *Hineni!*

Genesis 22 is the first time Abraham will answer, "Here I am!" He will say it three times in this chapter. The first time, we know that he is being tested. The idea of a test will come up again in scripture.

In the New Testament we read of Jesus being tested three times. The first time is in the wilderness when Satan tries to entice Him. Later He prays, "Lead me not into temptation, but deliver me from evil" (Matthew 6:13). Christ knows that the only way to affect the salvation of humanity is to suffer and die, to provide a way for all humanity through the Atonement. And finally, Christ is tested in Gethsemane. He asks that the cup, the test, be taken from Him if there is any other way.

God tells Abraham, "Take your son, your only son Isaac, whom you love, and go to the land of Moriah, and offer him there as a burnt offering one of the mountains I shall show you."

Abraham goes.

We should ask ourselves if our hero, Abraham, would ever sacrifice his child. Historically and biblically, we know human sacrifice was prohibited. There are many biblical warnings against human sacrifice. To our modern ears, we are shocked and more than uncomfortable. The ancients would have been, too. It's shocking, monstrous, and evil. We know that Abraham himself was offered as a sacrifice by his father (see Abraham 1:6–7). There is nothing so heinous, terrible, and wicked than this.

So Abraham arose early in the morning, saddled his donkey, and took two of his young men with him, as well as his son, Isaac. He cut the wood for the burnt offering and set out to the place in the distance that God had shown him.

Abraham shows no hesitation. He gets up early to obey.

When we are asked in faith to do something so hard, so inconceivable we don't have words, will we do it? How will we feel? Abraham's response raises the question that perhaps how we think about a divine command is not that important. But that seems to deny our agency, feelings, and morality.

We know that Abraham promptly obeys. What we don't know is how he feels, what his doubts and questions might be, his silent prayers as he takes the long three-day journey. We are forced to take the uncertain journey with them. We are unsettled and worried. Quiet and uneasy. We can almost feel the crunch of the ground beneath our feet and taste the fear and worry as Abraham slowly walks, trudging ever closer to the place.

"On the third day Abraham looked up and saw the place far away. Then Abraham said to his young men, 'Stay here with the donkey; the boy and I will go over there; we will worship, and then we will come back to you'" (NRSV, Genesis 22:4–5).

Alone the father and son must make the last of the journey. There is no going back. The servants are left behind, and there is no one to rescue Isaac or protest or step in at the last minute. The tension builds, and our thoughts race with questions the biblical account does not answer. We live the experience through Abraham's. There are times of trial and test in our lives when hope and answers seem far, far away. We walk alone. In fear, clinging to faith, we choose to obey. We choose to hope. We walk, one step at a time, towards the test.

"Abraham took the wood of the burnt offering and laid it on his son Isaac, and he himself carried the fire and the knife. So the two of them walked on together" ((NRSV, Genesis 22:6).

It is only the two of them now. Closer and closer to their fate, to the test.

"Isaac said to his father Abraham, 'Father!' And he said, 'Here I am, my son'" ((NRSV, Genesis 22:7).

Hineni!

For the second time in our story, Abraham is called. Isaac calls, "Father!" We can almost hear Abraham's voice break with emotion as he answers. "Behold, I am here. I am reminded that I am a father. I am the Father of Nations, the Exalted Father" (see Genesis 17:5). "And that this boy, this promised boy, is my beloved and promising child, my special son." Abraham is Isaac's father, and he loves this special boy.

"[Isaac] said, 'The fire and the wood are here, but where is the lamb for a burnt offering?' Abraham said, 'God himself will provide the lamb for the sacrifice, my son.' . . . So the two of them walked on together" (NRSV, Genesis 22:7–8.)

Does Isaac know? We can feel it. Isaac has figured out that he is to be the sacrifice. There is no lamb. It is him. Is it fear, disbelief, faith that tinges Isaac's voice? Abraham's answer can be read as the affirmative, that God will provide the sacrifice. Despite what they both know and fear, they continue to the test together.

"When they came to the place that God had shown him, Abraham built an altar there and laid the wood in order. He bound his son Isaac, and laid him on the altar, on top of the wood" (NRSV, Genesis 22:9).

Scholars have posited that Isaac was a young man, while Abraham was very old (Genesis 22:6). Isaac was young and strong, somewhere between twenty-seven and thirty-six years old. He must have submitted to Abraham's will. He was a willing sacrifice. And with trust in his eyes, Isaac let himself be bound.

"Then Abraham reached out his hand and took the knife to kill his son" (NRSV, Genesis 22:10).

The story must lead to this point. It is like we are watching all along. We are slowly zooming in. We go from the journey to the mountain. Then the father and son walking together. Finally, we see the altar, the wood, and the binding. Our view sharpens inward, being drawn to Abraham and his hand, and finally the knife. We are there, poised at the very moment, the knife raised, Isaac below, our fear and tension at its height.

The binding invites us into Abraham's test because we, too, will be tested. We are asked to do things we don't understand—scary things, outrageous things, challenging things, and, at times, things that are impossible to understand. When we don't grasp why God is asking this of us, we can be like Abraham. We can cry out, "Here I am! Here I am, Lord. I don't understand, and I cannot always understand. But I will do what you ask. I will have faith. I will take the test, and I will accept what you already know about me. I will prove it to myself. Here. I. Am."

"But the angel of the Lord called to him from heaven, and said, 'Abraham, Abraham!' And he said, 'Here I am'" (NRSV, Genesis 22:11).

For the third time, Abraham responds. "Here I am. Please, Lord, don't make me go through with it. Let this test pass. Save me, Lord. Please help me. I trust you can. I am here—save me."

> [The angel] said, "Do not lay your hand on the boy or do anything to him; for now I know that you fear God, since you have not withheld your son, your only son, from me." And Abraham looked up and saw a ram, caught in a thicket by its horns. Abraham went and took the ram and offered it up as a burnt offering instead of his son. So Abraham called that place "The Lord will provide"; as it is said to this day, "On the mount of the Lord it shall be provided." (NRSV, Genesis 22:12–14)

Abraham is saved. Isaac is saved. Abraham knows now that he loves his son. He doesn't just love Ishmael, but he loves Isaac as well. He knows what God knows, that he would obey Him. And we know that God Himself will prepare a sacrifice.

There is an example of a sacrifice that will carry the wood Himself. In this, we see a symbol of the great sacrifice of the Lamb. One day, the Father and the Son will walk together to that mount and provide salvation for all of us.

Because the story has so little description, it purposefully teaches us. And however we answer the many questions the narrative may provide, from the whys and hows, the motivations and the feelings, God is ever present in the story. We engage personally and emotionally in the story because there is so little detail. We enter the narrative and see our lives reflected in the scriptural account. There can be many applications, many conclusions. But we have only one clear conclusion: God keeps His covenant promises. He is aware of us and walks beside us during our trials. He will provide the sacrifice in our place.

Rather than a story of failure, it is a story of faith. It is a story of a test. It is a story of obedience.

It is a story of victory in our lives when we trust God.

It is a story of the test of life that we all must face. Will we face it with God, trusting Him despite any misgivings, fear, or doubt. When our steps falter, will we continue onward? When the thing we love the most is at risk, what will we choose? When God calls our name, how will we respond?

Hineni. Here I am, send me!

JACOB

Jacob is my favorite biblical hero. I know, I am probably not supposed to have a favorite, but I do. I can relate to Jacob. He goes through a remarkable change. His story is fascinating because while born to an amazing family with all the advantages, he is kind of a dork, a nerd, and a trickster. It is because he is a man with failings who overcomes that I love him. That guy, the one who tricks his brother and father, becomes a changed man and the father of a chosen nation. His story of change and redemption is one I can never get enough of.[1]

But I'm starting with the conclusion.

Let's start at the beginning.

A STORY IN THREE ACTS

Jacob's life is full challenge and change. His story is told in three acts. Like a movie, Jacob's life moves through three distinct phases. I know it is odd to think of scriptures like movies or fiction. The biblical authors are brilliant, geniuses, really. They take the events of history, when God worked with humanity, and carefully craft them so that we can see God's presence. In shaping the record into a story, they share eternal truths. They highlight events that we may not see otherwise. They draw attention to subtle clues of

---

1. I should let you in on a little secret. I love Jacob because he's a twin and so am I. Maybe you can relate. Maybe you have a scriptural character you have always seen yourself in. Mine is Jacob. You can like him, too. Ask yourself why you like the people you do. It might tell you a little about yourself.

God at work in their lives. They underscore eternal truths so we do not miss them. Like the prophet Mormon, carefully choosing from a room of records the stories of the Nephites,[2] we get the critical elements of the story that teach us of Christ.

ACT I: THE OLDER WILL SERVE THE YOUNGER

Like so many other stories of the matriarchs and patriarchs, Rebekah and Isaac cannot conceive. It is only through the intervention of God that a miracle, a child, is born. In this case, it's twins. Rebekah receives a revelation: "Two nations are in your womb, and two peoples from within shall be divided; the one shall be stronger than the other, and the older will serve the younger" (NRSV, Genesis 25:19).

Jacob's story starts before he is even born.

Primogeniture

Anciently there was a practice of primogeniture. Fundamentally, it was a law about inheritance. The firstborn son would receive the blessings of the priesthood (see Genesis 25:3, 25:31),[3] as well as a double portion of the earthly wealth, like land (see Deuteronomy 21:16). The promises of Abraham and Isaac would pass to the firstborn son. This means the priesthood, the promise of family, and a promised land. And through this family, all nations of the world would be blessed. The firstborn son was also dedicated to the Lord to remember the salvation of the Israelites from Egypt (see Exodus 13:11–15). This child would be the special ownership of the Lord. Not only would he receive the extra portion of the inheritance, but he would also be responsible for the family (see Genesis 48:22; Deuteronomy 21:17). Receiving the birthright meant

---

2. Mormon 1:5
3. Nahum M. Sarna, *Understanding Genesis* (New York: The Jewish Theological Seminary), 184.

receiving the covenant. It meant following the Lord and supporting and saving the family when they strayed. It came with extra material blessings so the firstborn son could redeem the family (pay for their debts when things went wrong). So, yes, the birthright came with inheritance, but it also came with a lot of responsibility. The older son was blessed so he could redeem his family.

What's in a Name?

While we have talked about names previously, in this story, the names tell us about the twin boys' character.[4] Their names are layered in meaning, their personalities, and their futures.

Esau is born first. His name means hairy or full-bodied. He is ruddy. The nature of his birth gives us clues into his personality and drives. He becomes a man of action, a man of the outdoors who hunts and follows his passions. Like an animal, Esau is characterized by the moment. His family becomes Israel's enemies, the Edomites, meaning red. We will see this reference to red again when Esau loses the birthright. The indication here is a hint, an indicator of this when he sells his birthright for a soup of red lentils.

Jacob is born second, holding onto the heel of his brother. His name means "he grabs the heel." In context, there is an idea of supplanting, usurping, or taking over. There is a lot wrapped up in this name, so let's take a minute to unpack it. A family probably wouldn't name their child a name like a usurper. Indeed, it seems that there is a positive connotation that 'aqab' is the idea of protection. For example, "following close behind." The idea is probably of

---

4. The name of the twins has special significance. Esau not only means hairy as stated in Genesis 25:25, but it also sounds like Edom. His descendants would settle there, so there is a play on words (Genesis 36:8–9). Esau is red, like 'ādōm (v. 30). In similar fashion, Jacob, ya'ăqōb, means "he grasps the heel" and supplants his older brother (Jeremiah 9:4). The word heel, 'āqēb, ties back to baby Jacob holding onto his brother's heel at birth. Similarly, the verb 'āqab means "deceived" (Genesis 27:36; Hosea 12:3–4).

God following close behind, to protect, *'y'qb-'l,* "may God protect." In this verse, the name is a bit of a play on words in Hebrew.

Heel = *'aqeb* and deceived = *'aqab'*. So the idea that Jacob, grasping Esau's heel at birth, is a deceiver and an opportunist. Hosea recounts this behavior as an example of how Jacob and the Israelites were defiant of the Lord and struggled to gain a blessing (see Hosea 12:2–4).[5]

That was a lot to unravel. Esau is passionate, Jacob is smooth and a trickster. Right from birth, from their names and descriptions, we set this up. Of course, in Hebrew, it wouldn't have needed an extensive explanation. It would have been evident and clever, but since we're here three thousand years later, we have to explain it.

In modern stories, we learn about people, their motivations, desires, and personality in detail. We may be given a flashback that highlights foundational events in a person's life. We might also hear a person's inner thoughts and desires. The biblical narrative is different. There is rarely a flashback or a conversation with friends highlighting their motivations. The scriptural stories use a different set of techniques. One of those is the person's name and physical description.

Actions and Outcomes

Another key to understanding scriptural characters is examining their actions and outcomes. Instead of understanding their inner motivations and monologues, we are left to look at what they do. When we see a person's actions or the results of their actions, we are supposed to make conclusions. When Rebekah immediately follows Eliezar to marry Isaac, we can conclude she is quick to obey. And when Ishmael teases a toddler, getting himself kicked out of the family, we understand he has ill intent for his little brother. Pay attention to these kinds of actions. The story of Jacob and Esau tells

---

5.   A. R. Millard, "Jacob" ISBE 2.948. See also: Mathews, K. A. Genesis 11:27–50:26. (United States: Broadman & Holman Publishers), 2005.

us a great deal but through consequences. It won't tell us definitively because we must make sense of it for ourselves. But it will give us something to consider, hints of meaning that we can try and understand.

Physical Descriptions

You have probably noticed there are not many physical descriptions of people in scripture. We don't know what Adam and Eve looked like—if Adam preferred a beard or Eve wore her hair up. We don't know if Lehi was a tall man or Sariah liked seafood. I am using ridiculous examples to prove a point. We rarely hear physical descriptions of people. So, when we do, it is critically important. For example, Nephi being larger than others shows us his spiritual strength (and how he can support his family, build a ship, and cross an ocean). Elijah and John the Baptist wear unique clothes, linking them in our minds (see 2 Kings 1:8; Matthew 3:4). Elijah was the prophet to turn the people back to the Lord, and John the Baptist held a similar calling. I think of them wearing a unique "prophet uniform" that indicated that they were particular prophets. Samson was powerful and had long hair as part of his Nazirite vow (see Numbers 6:1–21). Samson's strength was related to the covenants he made, part of his consecrated status to wear his hair long. Remembering that descriptions are few and far between, we turn back to the story of Jacob and Esau.

The Twins

The twins are opposites. Esau's name means hairy, and he is described as red and hairy, like a little animal (see Genesis 25:25). Later, we see his actions emphasize this. Esau is a hunter, and he is out "in the field" (Genesis 25:27). Jacob is the opposite, "a quiet man, living in tents" (27). It is easy to read through this quickly and assume it is just a little backstory, but it is the basis of the family fracture (spoiler alert). Instead of Esau receiving the birthright,

Jacob, the younger, will be chosen. Before their birth, the ground-work is set.

Esau is wild, active, and, shortly we'll find out, not interested in things of God. He marries two non-Israelite women. In sharp contrast to his parents, Rebekah and Isaac, who are partners and equals, Esau doesn't care at all. Later, we will see Jacob going to great lengths to find the right partner. In the next scene, Esau sells his birthright for some stew. Upon his arrival after hunting, he says, "I am famished . . . I am about to die!" That seems a bit extreme. Esau is uncontrolled, animalistic. Spiritual life holds no value. He is a man of passion, not patience. He doesn't value the birthright, but rather he barters it for lunch. One chapter later, we learn only one thing about Esau. He marries two women, both outside of the covenant, which does not go well. "And they made life bitter for Isaac and Rebekah" (Genesis 26:34–35). From his name and few actions, it is clear Esau is choosing everything other than God.

Jacob is more thoughtful. He is "smooth-skinned" (Genesis 27:11) but also "smooth" and clever-minded. He stays at home, implying he likes to study, read, and administer the house-hold. I'm not *actually* sure what "living in tents" means. It is the opposite of the outdoor, wild, hunting lifestyle of Esau. In my mind, Esau is an alpha male, enjoying sports and hunting. He is a man of action. Jacob is more of a book nerd, staying at home, not bothered doing administrative tasks, and learning to lead. I imagine Jacob as intelligent and dedicated. Jacob is much like Isaac, quiet and faithful. Perhaps this is why Isaac doesn't appreciate it (there's some psychology there, I'm sure). Both life choices are valid—either twin could have chosen God. Yet, in this characterization, Esau's out-ward actions and appearance tell us about his inner desires and motivations.

Set-up

From Rebekah's prophecy, to the twins fighting in the womb, to Esau devaluing the things of God, we see the two at odds for each other. That's when the first significant act of Jacob's life, receiving the birthright, occurs.

When Isaac gets old, he realizes he needs to bless his sons and confer the birthright. His age has gotten the best of him, and he is blind. He calls out to Esau and tells him about his intention to bless him. Isaac asks Esau to go hunting and bring him a special meal for the occasion. Esau leaves to hunt for the special dinner. Rebekah overhears the whole thing and devises a plan.

She works out a plan with Isaac to fool his blind father. Rebekah cooks a goat with the seasonings that Isaac likes. There is one other issue with this plan: Esau is hairy. Isaac will be able to tell Jacob is not Esau because his body is not hairy. Again, using the goat, Rebekah will disguise Isaac's skin with goat hair. While we know Esau sold his birthright for the stew earlier, the actual blessing from Isaac is still forthcoming. Isaac worries about it and says, "Perhaps my father will feel me, and I shall seem to be mocking him, and bring a curse on myself and not a blessing" (NRSV, Genesis 27:12).

They go through with the plan. Rebekah prepares a goat with special attention so it tastes like venison. Isaac puts the goat hair on his smooth skin to disguise himself as Esau. Jacob carries the meal into his father's tent and fools him. Then Jacob receives the blessing:

> "Ah, the smell of my son
> > is like the smell of a field that the Lord has blessed.
> May God give you of the dew of heaven,
> > and of the fatness of the earth,
> > nd plenty of grain and wine.
> Let peoples serve you,
> > and nations bow down to you.
> Be lord over your brothers,
> > and may your mother's sons bow down to you.
> Cursed be everyone who curses you,
> > and blessed be everyone who blesses you!"
> > (NRSV, Genesis 27:27–29)

Jacob receives the blessing of the birthright son. There are also echoes of the Abrahamic covenant: leadership, blessing, and prosperity. This is what was foretold before he was born. In the next chapter, Isaac is not deceived but blesses Jacob, showing us Isaac knew what Esau was. Isaac may have been fooled initially, but here we see Isaac is deliberate:

> May God Almighty bless you and make you fruitful and numerous, that you may become a company of peoples. May he give you the blessing of Abraham, to you and to your offspring with you, so that you may take possession of the land where you now live as an alien—land that God gave Abraham. (NRSV, Genesis 28:3–4)

Just when we think that it is going well, when a blessing of great worth is given, the story takes a turn. Esau receives a blessing but not the covenant. He is furious. He hates Jacob and plans on killing him. Jacob must flee for his life.

Jacob, as Imperfect Patriarch

Does it strike you as odd that one of the ancient patriarchs wanted to fool his father? It should. It should make us uncomfortable and ask questions. But right there, in verse 12, we see that Jacob knows it is a bad idea, that he feels guilt and is worried about what will happen: "Perhaps my father will feel me, and I shall seem to be mocking him, and bring a curse on myself and not a blessing" (NRSV, Genesis 27:12). Like him, we should hesitate, question this act, and search our feelings.

There's a thematic motif here that impacts additional generations. Jacob speaking about "a curse instead of a blessing" is prophetic. We are going to see Jacob run for his life. As a result, he lives outside of the promised land for decades. He fools his aging father, and later, he will be tricked by his wife and father-in-law. The fooling and deceit stay with the family. Later, Jacob's sons fool him about killing Joseph. They cover his unique coat with the blood of a goat. That goat is a thematic element, so there is no doubt of the connection. Jacob deceives, and that deception follows him. From Rebekah to Jacob, Laban, to Judah and Joseph, the deceit follows the family. Like an infection, it takes a while to heal. Jacob's sins rebound on him.

Jacob is imperfect. He fools his brother and tricks his father. What are we to make of this? For now, in this part of the story, we take note. We realize that Jacob has made some tough choices. He is setting the path of his character. Will this be who Jacob is? Is Jacob a deceiver, focused on only himself? What if what he wants is a good thing? Does doing something bad for a good reason ever make sense?

We must continue with the story to find out.

ACT II: VISION AND COVENANT

Jacob's sins drive him out. He flees his actions and his brother, Esau. He is in spiritual darkness. He is alone, driven from home and family, support, and protection. He has "gained" the blessing, but at what cost? While the Lord is not deceived and Isaac confirms the blessing, the event leaves us uncomfortable. Jacob begins his journey, not only an actual, physical event but also a symbolic one. Jacob has a choice to determine what kind of person he will be. Just like in Jacob's figurative landscape, the sun sets and darkness settles in. Alone, in the dark, he sleeps.

Jacob has a dream.

Jacob's Ladder

Jacob sees a ladder, a tower or ramp, reaching into heaven with its base on earth.[6] Angels are going up and down into heaven on the ramp. The Lord stands next to him and says,

---

6. Warren C. Trenchard. סֻלָּם *A Concise Dictionary of the Words in the Greek New Testament and The Hebrew Bible (Cambridge: 2003),* See entry 5551 (1) and 5551. סֻלָּם *cullâm, sool-lawm ́; from 5549; a stair-case:—ladder.*

"I am the Lord, the God of Abraham your father and the God of Isaac; the land of which you lie I will give to you and to your offspring; and your offspring shall be like the dust of the earth, and you shall spread abroad to the west and to the east and to the north and to the south; and all the families of the earth shall be blessed in you and in your offspring. Know that I am with you and will keep you wherever you go and will bring you back to this land; for I will not leave you until I have done what I have promised you." (NRSV, Genesis 28:12–15)

Jacob awakens and praises God. He realizes that God is close, present in the world. He had rested against a stone, so to commemorate the place, Jacob pours oil on it and names it Bethel, House of God.

Rather than a distant Creator, the Lord is deeply involved in supporting and loving Jacob and all of us. Despite Jacob's actions, God will support him, bless him, and help him become the man He knows Jacob can be. Jacob realizes that there are places where heaven and Earth meet, like a hotspot, a place where the veil is thin. The celestial realm is close, much closer than he ever expected. Jacob can see that life is much more than what is visible to him.

Jacob has made a covenant. The Lord has bound Himself to Jacob, and Jacob learns that He is near. There, when all seems dark and Jacob is alone, he learns that God is close. In Bethel, the house of God, he understands that despite his failings, the promises of God are powerful, near, and present.

Jacob Struggles

After his vision at Bethel, Jacob continues to the land of his mother. He meets Rachel, with whom he falls in love. Jacob works for years to earn her hand. Rachel's father, Laban, tricks Jacob into marrying Leah, his older daughter. Because of the deceit, Jacob works for seven additional years to marry both of Laban's daughters. Leah, whom he does not love, bears many children. Rachel is barren. In desperation, she gives her maid to Jacob as a wife. Leah does so in turn. Over and over, Rachel cannot conceive, and Leah and the two maids, Bilhah and Zilpah, have children. At this stage of his life, Jacob struggles with his father-in-law. Disputes about business and religion arise. From family to business, Jacob's life is one of deception and conflict. Struggle and strife underscore his life. At long last, Rachel conceives and has a son, Joseph. Soon after the birth, Jacob decides to move back to his ancestral home.

In Act II, Jacob is no longer the young man. He has changed and matured. He has gained experience and been humbled by life. He can see the results of deceit and has been the recipient of its effects. It is a long story with twists and turns, lessons, and insights. Despite the many lessons he has had and the struggle with family, he has not fully turned to God. That is about to change.

ACT III: REDEMPTION

Jacob fears as he returns to Canaan, the promised land. He is returning to the place where he made mistakes and where his brother, Esau, still lives. While we do not know what he is feeling, his actions tip us off.

Before Jacob returns home, he sends special messengers ahead to warn Esau he is returning. He also sends the message, "Thus says your servant Jacob, 'I have lived with Laban as an alien, and stayed until now; and I have oxen, donkeys, flocks, male and female slaves; and I have sent to tell my lord, in order that I may find favor in your sight'" (NRSV, Genesis 32:4–5).

This is a different Jacob. He tells Esau that he is "his servant." The Jacob who fooled his brother has grown up, matured, and repented. He doesn't know what kind of man Esau has grown to be. He fears the worst. It seems his fears are confirmed when Jacob's messengers return and inform him that Esau has a massive party of four hundred men with him. This sounds like a small army. Esau could kill Jacob and his whole family. Esau was very rash when he was younger and threatened to kill him. Jacob splits up his family into two groups so if there is an attack half will survive.

Can you imagine? We all have family fights. But can you imagine fearing for the life of your spouse and children? This is a tense situation. Jacob fears Esau with real fear. He fears for his family. He fears for his own life. He forwards on many flocks and herds as a gift to Esau, hoping to smooth out the issues. Jacob tells his servant, "And you shall say, 'Moreover your servant Jacob is behind us.'" For he thought, "I may appease him with the present that goes ahead of me, and afterwards I shall see his face; perhaps he will accept me" (NRSV, Genesis 32:20).

Then Jacob prays. We can feel the fear and the worry Jacob has for his family. What will Esau do? In his prayer, Jacob asks for protection. Then, sending his family up ahead, he prepares to meet Esau across the river Jabbok.

Alone, in the dark, he crosses the river to meet his fate.

Jacob Wrestles an Angel

As the darkness descends and Jacob is there alone, a mysterious figure, a representative of God, meets him. And there, they wrestle.

> The same night he got up and took his two wives, his two maids, and his eleven children, and crossed the ford of the Jabbok. He took them and sent them across the stream, and likewise everything that he had. Jacob was left alone; and a man wrestled with him until daybreak. When the man saw that he did not prevail against Jacob, he struck him on the hip socket; and Jacob's hip was put out of joint as he wrestled with him. Then he said, "Let me go, for the day is breaking." But Jacob said, "I will not let you go, unless you bless me." So he said to him, "What is your name?" And he said, "Jacob." hen the man said, "You shall no longer be called Jacob, but Israel, for you have striven with God and with humans, and have prevailed." Then Jacob asked him, "Please tell me your name." But he said, "Why is it that you ask my name?" And there he blessed him. So Jacob called the place Peniel, saying, "For I have seen God face to face, and yet my life is preserved." The sun rose upon him as he passed Penuel, limping because of his hip. (NRSV, Genesis 32: 22–31)

Jacob wrestles an angel (an angel is a special messenger representing the Lord Himself). They contend all night. During this match, Jacob's hip is wrenched.

The angel says, "Let me go."

"I will not. Unless you bless me."

The angel then asks Jacob his name. Upon hearing it, the angel says, "Your name will no longer Jacob, because you have striven with God and prevailed" (Genesis 32:26–28).

Jacob later names the place *Peniel*, for, "I have seen a divine being and prevailed" (NRSV, Genesis 32:20). Then, the sun rises.

Light and Dark

Darkness is mentioned four times in just a few verses. You'll remember Jacob left the promised land at night. It is as if that dark part of Jacob's life can now be put behind him. The wrestle, the struggle with himself, is over. He leaves in darkness, but a new man emerges—a humble servant of God who chooses to follow the Lord through struggle. Then, a new dawn arises.

Change in the Lord

Names are important. This clue to understanding character cannot be overemphasized. This time, this most important event, the giving of a new name, shows us the very essence of the bearer.[7] By naming something or knowing the name of something gives you insights into them. That's why the angel won't reveal his name—it would give power and authority over him. It is also why Israelites and even Jews today do not say or write the name of God. To keep it sacred, to show reverence, they do not speak or write the name of the Divine.

This day, Jacob does give his own name. And that's when he receives a new name: Israel, which means "one who is wrestled with

7. Nahum M. Sarna, *Understanding Genesis* (New York: The Jewish Theological Seminary), 130.

the Lord," "one who strives with God," or "God strives" (Genesis 32:20).

Jacob, once the deceiver and usurper, has, with God, become someone new. Did you catch the name of the river—Jabbok? It is a bit of a pun, with the names Jacob and Jabbok sounding so similar. But it reminds us about Jacob's character. He can choose to be Jacob or something else. We, too, can cross over, leaving the old self behind. We can wrestle with our old self, the parts of us that we do not like. When we hold fast to the Lord and never let go, we can prevail.

The angel of the Lord has told him that he prevails because he has wrestled and prevailed. Jacob has overcome his inner challenges. After a life that began with deceit, he is humble. He learns as a unique being, and he will exercise his free will. Jacob chooses now to follow God. He becomes a man of faith, an individual of humility. He withstood the trial, and he's obedient. Once he struggled with who he used to be, but he changed his heart. Jacob represents someone who God can change. He gives up his old self and, in the Lord, becomes something greater.

Jacob, now Israel, is changed and humbled. He literally limps into the promised land.

BIG WRAP-UP

President Russell M. Nelson said,

Jacob proved what was most important to him. He demonstrated that he was willing to let God prevail in his life. . . . Are *you* willing to let God prevail in your life? Are *you* willing to let God be the most important influence in your life? Will you allow His words, His commandments, and His covenants to influence what you do each day? Will you allow His voice to take priority over any other? Are you *willing* to let whatever He needs you to do take precedence over every other ambition? Are you *willing* to have your will swallowed up in His?[8]

Jacob's story is our story. We will make mistakes. Like him, we may have troubles with our family or those closest to us. It may be that we desire to do the right things but still struggle to let God prevail in our lives. We receive power and strength as we remember our covenants. We prevail at the House of the Lord, Bethel, and witness how thin the veil is. We continue, like Jacob, along the covenant path, and ultimately, when we give all we are to Him, He can make us a new person. And a new dawn rises in our lives.

In the October 2021 general conference, President Russell M. Nelson extended this challenge to all of us: "So I ask of each of you, how firm is *your* foundation? And what reinforcements to your testimony and understanding of the gospel are needed?"[9] We are being asked to reinforce our testimonies, our knowledge of the gospel of Jesus Christ. Like Jacob, we may have some cracks, our foundation may have settled, and it is time to sure up our foundations. By returning to our covenants, specifically in the House of the Lord, we can reinforce our understanding of the Lord. Again, our beloved prophet said,

> The temple lies at the center of strengthening our faith and our fortitude because the Savior and His doctrine are the very heart of the temple. Everything taught in the temple, through instruction and through the Spirit, increases our understanding of Jesus Christ. His essential ordinance bind us to Him through sacred priesthood covenants. Then, as we keep our covenants, He endows us with His healing, strengthening power. And oh, how we will need His power in the days ahead.[10]

---

8. Russell M. Nelson, "Let God Prevail" *Liahona,* November 2020.
9. Russell M. Nelson, "The Temple and Your Spiritual Foundation" *Liahona,* November, 2021.
10. Ibid.,

I love the story of Jacob, the twin, the one who wrestles with God, because ultimately, he does it! Jacob isn't a hero because he never makes mistakes. Jacob is a hero because, with the Savior, he overcomes his mistakes. He is a hero despite his sins, his errors, and his bad decisions. Jacob never gives up. He keeps fighting, keeps wrestling. Jacob, forever Israel, has chosen to let God prevail.

THE DELIVERERS

Moses, Miriam, and Aaron

THREE DELIVERERS

The deliverance of the house of Israel from bondage, oppression, and slavery in Egypt is epic. It frames the people of Israel into a nation, a people under God's direction. Four of the first five books of the Bible tell the story. Jesus Christ refers to the law, these stories, as critical to His gospel. His most famous sermons, including the Sermon on the Mount, Sermon on the Plain, and Sermon at the Temple, build on Moses's principles and rules on Sinai.[1] Jesus famously answered which was the greatest commandment with, "Love the Lord your God with all your heart and with all your soul and all your mind. This is the first and greatest commandment. All the law and the prophets hang on these two commandments" (Matthew 22:37–40). The Lord understood the law as a central part of scripture, and it continues as vital and alive today.

The story of the Exodus is not just a story of epic miracles. It contains the law. Surprisingly, the law is not a list of rules and statutes. The law is a group of instructions and teachings wrapped in stories. The word in Hebrew, *Torah*, means precisely that—instruction. (*Torah* is the name of the first five books of the Bible

---

1. Sermon on the Mount: Matthew 5–7: Sermon on the Plain: 6:20–49; and Sermon at the Temple: 3 Nephi 12–16, 20–22.

in Hebrew).[2] The pattern is repeated over and over. We will get the record of regular people, and then when something happens, God will reveal some rules for how to behave and treat each other. The law is about people like you and me and how they stumble, even utterly fail, and God shows them a higher, holier way. A key, then, to understanding the law is to understand the stories that prompt the commandments.

The story of the Exodus (and Leviticus, Numbers, and Deuteronomy) is a story of three siblings—two brothers and a sister. Each has their own failings and their own successes. They each encounter God and choose to serve Him. As they put their trust in Him, God changes them. God works with them, and they become more faithful and more effective. But I'm jumping to the end. Let's start at the beginning. This is the story of Moses, Miriam, and Aaron.

BACKGROUND

After God chooses the family of Abraham to bestow His covenant, the family grows. From Abraham, the covenant is passed to Isaac, and from Isaac to Jacob. (There's a whole section of the book on this period, so reread that if you need a refresher). Jacob has twelve sons, one of whom is Joseph. Joseph is sold into Egypt as a slave by his brothers. He suffers, but eventually, through his divine gifts, he rises until he is second in command to Pharaoh. As famine strikes the land, the brothers come to Egypt. After a series of incredible events, the family is restored. In Egypt they thrive and grow.

Four hundred years later, a pharaoh arises that doesn't know Joseph. The Israelites have grown into a vast people. To control them, Pharaoh puts them under servitude and slavery.

---

2. F. Brown, S. Driver, and C. Briggs, *The Brown-Driver-Briggs Hebrew and English Lexicon* (Boston: Hendrickson Publishers, 2004), 8451.

PHARAOH

Pharaoh is the horrifying villain of the book of Exodus. Earlier in the Bible, we meet other big bad characters like Cain, who killed his brother. Soon after the story of fratricide, we meet Lamech. Lamech chants about killing a boy just for being annoying, and he controls his wives like property. He is truly terrible. Later, the entire nation of Babel, also called Babylon, rises in opposition to the Lord. Babylon is a nation of unfaithful people. Yet, we have never met anyone as genuinely awful as Pharaoh. Here on the mighty Nile River banks, we meet the biggest, baddest villain so far in the Bible. He is so evil we don't give him a name. He is a man without remorse or kindness and is not deserving of a name. We will only ever call him by a title. While he was a real man in ancient times, he also reflects our time. He represents all that was evil then and now. By not naming him, we can see Pharaoh in all those who oppress and hate. Pharaoh is the representative of the evil of power, tyranny, and hatred. He is oppression, murder, and terror all wrapped into one.

SET-UP

The Israelites have grown into an enormous number of people. They are so large that they threaten Pharaoh and his control of the nation. He makes them slaves and oppresses them, working them cruelly to control them. The Israelites build cities, and despite the slavery, they continue to grow. Pharaoh devises a plan more evil and more sinister than just slavery. He decides to have all the baby boys killed and orders them to be thrown into the Nile.

During this time of slavery and servitude, the Lord raises three deliverers. They are all from the same family, the children of Amram and Jochebed. Once again, God shows us deliverance by choosing a family. There is a common theme of God saving his entire family by starting with one. Adam and Eve, Abraham, and now Moses are all families that God chooses to save. There is an important theme, a literary motif in families. Perhaps God is trying to show us that we are His family and He will save us.

In this family, there are three children. The first is Miriam, then Aaron, and finally little Moses. Miriam is about ten years old, and Aaron is seven years younger. They are just little kids when baby Moses is born under this edict of death. Each will be deliverers, saviors of their people. But first, they must grow up.

KINGS AND BABIES

The story of Pharaoh is echoed in the New Testament, too. While Pharaoh's edict to kill the baby boys is to control the population, a king will threaten another baby. When Jesus is born, Herod, the puppet king of Rome, is afraid of another king supplanting him. He, too, orders the boys' death. Both Moses and Jesus, tiny babies, threaten the power of great kings. Both Jesus Christ and Moses will deliver their people. Now, back to the story of Moses, Aaron, and Miriam.

A DESPERATE PLAN AND A TINY ARK

Moses is born. His parents see that he is special. The scripture says, "When she [Moses's mother, Jochebed] saw him and that he was *tov* she hid him three months" (NRSV, Exodus 2:2). In Hebrew, the word is *tov* means good.[3] It is the same word Genesis uses to describe the Creation. Each act is *tov* until the Creation is complete, and then it is very *tov*, or very good. Jochebed sees that Moses is good—exceptional—and we see God's hand at work. Jochebed also loves her child and risks everything by hiding Moses. When he is three months old, the parents can no longer hide him. They devise a plan. They create an ark, a tiny basket of reeds.

---

3.   Ibid., 2896.

The Ark

We've heard the term *ark* before. In Genesis 7, the Lord commands Noah to create a wooden boat called an ark to deliver and save another family. The ark for Moses and Noah is the same word. We're supposed to see the connection. Even though one is large and one tiny, they are both wooden boats. In both instances, a family, a people, needs rescuing. God creates a way, through an ark, to save them. Why an ark, you ask?

An ark reminds us of a tree, an extraordinary tree at the beginning of the story of Creation. There, in the Garden of Eden, there are two trees—the tree of the knowledge of good and evil and the tree of life. Both are set right in the middle of Eden. They are central to the story. They are not shoved off to the side or hidden in the back behind other trees. They are in the very center and are "central" to the story.

The garden is a story of choice and life, agency, and salvation. Adam and Eve, and all of us, chose knowledge. That knowledge means we will fail, sin, and eventually die. But our Father has made a way to return to His presence, return to Eden, through the tree of life. We see this tree, an *etz* in Hebrew, a tree, bush, or wood, over and over again.[4] First it is in Eden. Later, a "converted" tree, an ark, saves Noah and humanity. Now, Moses is saved in another little tree. It is too bad this gets translated as "basket" because then we miss the connection. Forget basket and think ark.

In just a few chapters, God will appear in a burning bush, a small tree, to help redeem and save the people. Once again, in a particular place where heaven and earth meet, God appears to save and redeem His people. The burning bush reminds us of the tree of life in Eden. A few chapters later, the tables of the law and other miraculous items are put in a wooden box, an ark, and placed in the Holy of Holies in the tabernacle or temple. What's the name of that special ark? The ark of the covenant. Also, critically, the

---

4. Ibid., 3318.

ark is named the mercy seat. All the trees and arks point to God's plan to save. The tree of life in the garden was part of the plan all along to save humanity. It was there, all along, in the center of the garden. God created a tree to save us. How do we know? Finally, God Himself died on a tree, a cross, to save us all.

Now, back to *this* ark—a tiny, floating tree of life and the deliverer inside.

MOSES

Who is this boy that will save a nation? His name is Moses, which has a double meaning. In Hebrew, it sounds like the Hebrew verb "to draw out." The drawing out of water is not only what Pharaoh's daughter does from the Nile but also what Moses will do with the children of Israel. Moses will draw them out of the sea. The name Moses has a double meaning. An Egyptian naming convention with *mose* sounds like "to bear or give birth to."[5] The Egyptians would combine that name with the name of a god, like the sun-god Re or Thoth. Put the two together, and you get "the sun-god Re has given birth to him." Perhaps something like "Son of Thoth." We are more familiar with them as Re-moses or Rameses. Even Thoth-moses or Tutmoses, like King Tut.[6] Moses's name, then, is a perfect reflection of his two people. He is "Drawn Out" for the Hebrews and "Son of" a god for the Egyptians. Moses is unique, a man between two nations.

Moses's life consists of three parts. Each one is broken up in forty years.

- Part I: Prince of Egypt
- Part II: The Prophet, the Shepherd
- Part III: Israel's Leader, the Lawgiver

---

5. James K. Hoffmeier, *Israel in Egypt* (Oxford, England: Oxford University Press, 1999), 138–140.
6. Billauer, Barbara P., "Moses, the Tutmoses and the Exodus" (SSRN: April 25, 2014).

Each segment of Moses's life is characterized by events that teach him and mold him into something God can use. First, he is the Prince of Egypt, learning administration, war, and politics. The second phase of his life is spent in Midian. His life resets after leaving Egypt. He meets his wife, Zipporah, and starts a family, having at least two sons. He also learns of God. There, under the direction of Jethro, the priest of Midian, Moses lives the life of a shepherd. He learns to serve and to follow the ways of God. Finally, he returns as Israel's prophet and lawgiver, the servant whom God has chosen to deliver His people.

Each part of Moses's life lasts forty years, making him one hundred twenty years old. While people lived long lives in Old Testament times, Moses's age may be symbolic. The number forty can also be representative of a period of trial or testing.[7] It rained for forty days and forty nights as the world and Noah's faith were tested (see Genesis 7:12). Later, in Exodus, Moses will fast for forty days before ascending Sinai, a time of preparation for making a covenant (see Exodus 34:28). Jesus went into the wilderness, where He fasted for forty days, preparing for His mortal mission. Moses's age is not our focus. Instead, in each phase of his life, we see how God prepares him for the final role as prophet.

PART I: THE PRINCE OF EGYPT

Moses Kills an Egyptian

Moses's story is massive in scope and comprises a significant portion of the Old Testament. We could write volumes about his life, speeches, miracles, and impact. I know, I keep saying that, but it is true. The events and effects of the Exodus change Israel forever. It is impossible to overstate its impact. I can't possibly do all that

---

7. Alonzo L. Gaskill, *The Lost Language of Symbolism* (Salt Lake City: Deseret Book Company, 2003), 137.

in one book. Since we are looking at how God uses real people and real experiences, good and bad, let's just look at one short example of Moses.

After Moses's auspicious beginning, being saved in an ark, watched over by his sister, Miriam, and raised in the daughter of Pharaoh's house, we don't hear much about him. We know Moses grows up in the Egyptian court. But there is nothing else about those first forty years—no stories about his life as an Egyptian or a Hebrew. The lack of information serves a narrative purpose. It tells us that his life began when he met the Lord. The events that shaped him, and a nation, start now. Only after a significant action does Moses's biography begin.

The next impactful event recorded after Moses's rescue in the ark is Moses's killing of an Egyptian. Just the event, a murder, probably causes us concern. It should, at least, have us pull up a bit, raise an eyebrow, or purse our lips. This is the great Deliverer killing a human. Yet here it is, the first story we have of Moses as an adult. Let's unpack it and see if anything about this event tells us why it is included here.

Moses Makes Mistakes

One of the great strengths of scripture is that we hear about the characters honestly. We see their failures right along with their strengths. Other ancient Near Eastern accounts portrayed characters as nearly perfect, in unrealistically good ways.[8] Egypt and its surrounding areas showed their leaders as exceptional in every way. Scripture is the opposite. We get the good and the bad, the mistakes with the victories. It can be tempting to defend every action. We could say, "The Egyptian deserved it," or, "It was in self-defense." Or we could completely miss the point and say, "If (insert name

---

8. T. Butler, "An Anti-Moses Tradition," *JSOT* 12 [1979]: 9–15). Cf. also B. Childs, "Moses's Slaying in the Theology of the Two Testaments," in *Biblical Theology in Crisis* (Philadelphia: Westminster, 1970), 164–83.

here) did it, it must have been good because it is in the Bible." There are certainly some cases of actions being taken that are defensible, like Nephi killing Laban and acquiring the brass plates. However, I propose that the strength of some of these stories is that the biblical accounts have *real* people. These actual people learn from their mistakes or are cautionary tales of what we should avoid, like the entire book of Judges. The power of these stories is that the people are fallible, faulty, and imperfect, just like us.

> One day, after Moses had grown up, he went out to his people and saw their forced labor. He saw an Egyptian beating a Hebrew, one of his kinsfolk. He looked this way and that, and seeing no one he killed the Egyptian and hid him in the sand. (NRSV, Exodus 2:11–12)

Have you ever wondered if Moses felt more Egyptian or Hebrew? Movies like *The Ten Commandments* and musicals like *The Prince of Egypt* may have confused me over the years. They show Moses being surprised he is Hebrew. The biblical story shows something else entirely. While he is mistaken as an Egyptian when he first arrives in Midian, presumably from his speech and dress (see Exodus 2:19), he identifies with the Israelites. They are his people. And it shows us something powerful about Moses's role as a deliverer.

In just two verses, Moses sees the oppression of his people: "He went out to *his* people and saw *their* forced labor." Again, "one of his kinsfolk." These verses show us how Moses feels about the Israelites—he is one of them. Moses sees himself as an Israelite, not an Egyptian. He is witnessing the cruelty to his people for years, and he not only identifies with them, but it also builds a rage in him. Upon seeing the inhumanity and malice, he kills the Egyptian. Also, there is an insightful phrase included in the story. It says he "looks this way and that." This isn't just impulse but a plan, even if it is just a very quickly formulated plan. The following verses tell us he thinks he was unseen.

When he went out the next day, he saw two Hebrews fighting; and he said to the one who was in the wrong, "Why do you strike your fellow Hebrew?" He answered, "Who made you a ruler and a judge over us? Do you mean to kill me as you killed the Egyptian?" Then Moses was afraid and thought, "Surely the thing is known." When Pharaoh heard of it, he sought to kill Moses. But Moses fled from Pharaoh. (NRSV, Exodus 2:13–15)

Moses knows what he has done is wrong—he covers it up. People don't cover up things they think are just and proper. But, if these two Hebrews knew of it, then others would, too. The Israelites even question him in breaking up the fight, "Who made you the boss? The judge of us?" They are snarky, but a few interesting clues arise. They don't see Moses as a leader, their boss, nor any kind of judge.[9] This theme will resurface over and over with the Israelites learning how to follow. Moses has not only killed a man, but he has also buried him in the sand.[10] Far from helping the Israelites, Moses realizes he has only made it worse. The Israelites, and Moses, could be severely punished when it is discovered. What started as an attempt to save someone has turned into a mess, causing more damage to him and his people.

Moses Tries Deliverance on His Own

Moses defends one of his people. He attempts to save someone on his own. He is trying to be a deliverer, a savior, but he does it on his terms. He is not relying on God but his own strength. He acts alone and in secret. He uses his power, thoughts, and plans to defend his people. He does not turn to God. Rather than help

---

9. Hb. עָשָׁל, lit., "the guilty one," probably is a normal legal term, our equivalent of "the guilty party."

10. Exodus 9:12–21, 17:3; Numbers 14:2, Deuteronomy 1:27, The Israelites rejected leadership, whether it was the Lord or His representative. In the killing of the Egyptian, there may have been other motives, such as he was not actually their leader. Later, however, they still pushed back. What does this tell us about ourselves?

anyone, this action sends him in the wrong direction. While Moses identified with the Israelites, he grew up apart from them. They did not appreciate him and resented it.

There's a message in here. When we make mistakes, even as big as this one, God can turn it for our good. Murder is terrible. Yet, out of this disaster, God can do something. He can use it to change Moses if Moses lets it. However, Moses does not recognize it at the time—he must flee for his life! This act drives him from his home, his family, and both of his cultures. Moses wanted to defend one of his people from being beaten. I love that about him. He is stepping in to protect someone. It is difficult to see that this action changes Moses's direction. This mistake doesn't have to ruin Moses. Instead, the Lord uses it and teaches Moses to leave behind the Egyptians and start over, in the desert, as a shepherd. Because of the killing, Moses resets his life, and there he meets God.

Moses's Life after Egypt

We know a few critical events after Moses leaves Egypt. He flees to Midian, where he defends Jethro's family at a well. Moses marries Zipporah, has children, and eventually goes to Sinai. There he sees God, receives his mission, and returns to save the Israelites. When Moses returns to Egypt, he is a different man. He has seen the Lord; he comes as a deliverer in the strength of the Lord. Shortly, we'll hear Moses's Song of the Sea in which he praises God as a savior, a warrior, his salvation. But Moses does not do all this saving and delivering alone. He has help from his sister and brother.

Miriam's Story

Miriam is the oldest child of Amram and Jochebed, Israelites born amongst slavery and servitude. When we first meet her, she's nameless. It isn't that she does not have a name. It is just that we are not told it yet. We are introduced to Miriam as part of this great developing story about deliverance. When we first meet her, she is just part of this grand epic. We are not told her name because her story isn't the focus, at least not yet. But before we jump into Miriam's story, let's review the big picture. The story of the Exodus is God's story of salvation and freedom.

The Exodus

Miriam's story is set during a greater sweep of history. She is just part of this great developing story of God's deliverance. The theme of redemption is repeated over and over. For Jews and Christians, the Exodus is one of the foundational stories in all of scripture. Celebrated and retold as often as the Passover and Exodus, few scriptural stories are discussed, explained, celebrated, and referenced. As a sign of Christ's ultimate sacrifice and redemption of all humanity, the Exodus is a story of salvation. It is an event that is going to be celebrated even today, as the Passover. Jews today, and continually for over three thousand years, have celebrated the Passover to remember the miracles of these days of wonder. Christians celebrate it in its updated form, Easter and Resurrection Sunday.

From the Passover to the Red Sea, the Plagues of Egypt, to Mount Sinai, the events of the Exodus impact future prophets and people. Jesus, Matthew, Paul, Nephi, and Alma all quote from Exodus. We have seen the stories in film, musicals, and popular culture. While the stories are so grand and unique, we wonder how to apply those scriptures today.

Prophets will retell the story for centuries. Jeremiah, Ezekiel, and Hosea all refer to these critical events, showing God's promise of deliverance. Isaiah retells the salvation of the Hebrews as God's overcoming of tyranny. Book of Mormon prophets see their travels into the wilderness as a motif of the Exodus. Nephi, Alma, and Limhi recall the Israelite deliverance as a shadow of their own.[11] The New Testament prophet John the Baptist returns to Jordan to refresh the

---

11. S. Kent Brown, "The Exodus Pattern in the Book of Mormon," *From Jerusalem to Zarahemla: Literary and Historical Studies of the Book of Mormon* (Provo, UT: Religious Studies Center, Brigham Young University, 1998), 75–98.

crossing of the sea, a new birth for the house of Israel. The story of deliverance is recounted in Acts 7. And the Passover meal is recast as the sign of the new covenant of the Lord's Supper (see Luke 22:20). We, too, celebrate in the form of Easter, a commemoration of the atoning sacrifice and resurrection of our Lord. Christ's resurrection will be reframed as part of a new Exodus, a new deliverance.

We retell these stories because they are our stories. The story of the Passover is God's promise of salvation. In the escape and Exodus from Egypt, we see our escape from the oppression of death and sin. In the promised land, we welcome returning to God's presence and finally being accepted into His rest. In the Exodus, we see the entire plan of salvation of Jesus Christ.

It is also the story of individuals. The story of the Passover, the Exodus, begins with a baby boy protected by a girl. The story of salvation can take place on a grand scale with entire nations. God also saves one at a time. Miriam's story is the story of deliverance, one child, one person, one woman at a time.

Miriam Guards Baby Moses

Jochebed creates a little ark made of papyrus and places Moses inside. Then, putting him in the Nile among the reeds, she hopes her baby will live. Miriam, then just a young girl, watches and guards him. The Nile is no safe place. It's dangerous and wild, inhabited by some of the most ferocious beasts. Animals like crocodiles and hippos roam the banks. Hippos seem safe, but more people die from hippos in Africa than lions. There are also snakes living between the reeds that could kill a child instantly. Yet, this young girl braves the water and the animals to watch the baby. Amram, Jochebed, and Miriam place Moses in God's hands and hope. Here is where we meet Miriam, our hero.

A Tiny Deliverer

Miriam, unnamed at this point, is asked to watch over and guard baby Moses in this tiny ark. There among the wild beasts and Egyptian guards, she watches and hopes. Then, something surprising and unexpected happens. Pharaoh's daughter arrives! She sees a basket out in the Nile's reeds and sends her maid out to get it.

When the princess opens the ark, she discovers a crying baby. "This must be one of the Hebrews' children," she says.

With maturity and bravery, little Miriam approaches Pharaoh's daughter and asks, "Shall I go and get you a nurse from the Hebrew woman to nurse the child for you?"

At ten years old, Miriam, a slave, helps save Moses and cleverly allows her mother to continue raising Moses. She is our first deliverer, saving not only a baby but, in turn, an entire nation. We don't hear much of Miriam for the next forty years. Instead, the story turns to God saving the Israelites, and all of us, through the story of Moses. We even hear a little about Aaron, Miriam's other brother. Miriam's story doesn't end here, however. It carries through most of the following books of the Bible. We hear more about her in the later parts of the books of Exodus and Numbers.

PART II: THE PROPHET, THE SHEPHERD

Moses and Aaron

Moses has an older brother, Aaron. While Miriam saved Moses as a baby, Aaron will support him as an adult. Aaron enters the scene after Moses meets God on Sinai.

A Mountain, a Vision, a Calling

We have seen Miriam's role and Moses's beginning, but what of Aaron? In Exodus 3, Moses ascends Mount Horeb (also called Sinai) and has a vision. God tells Moses that the Israelite oppression by Egypt will soon come to an end. Moses learns God's name and is instructed to bring Israel to the mountain, to know and worship Him. God gives Moses some instructions and some signs that he can use to show God's calling and power. Then, an exciting interaction happens. Moses tells God, "No."

Slow of Speech

No is a strong word. Perhaps it is better to say Moses has doubts about his abilities. After receiving a calling to go to Egypt and bring the Israelites out, Moses says, "O my Lord, I am not eloquent, neither before nor since You have spoken to Your servant; but I am slow of speech and slow of tongue" (NRSV, Exodus 4:10).

It is interesting that Moses, after seeing the power and might of God, expresses doubt in himself. Or is it? I think we all imagine we will always be receptive and anxious to do God's commands. It is easy to believe that we would not hesitate to obey if we received a divine calling. Maybe we would, but perhaps, we are more like Moses. Moses has humility, he knows his human failings, and he has real concerns. Perhaps Moses is not doubting God. He doubts himself. At this point, Moses still sees himself apart from God. He knows he has weaknesses, specifically in speaking, and he fears the outcome.

How often do we do that? When God asks us to do something, we fear our weaknesses. We have yet to learn that with God, all things are possible.[12] Now, at this moment, Moses knows he is "slow of speech" and fears the confrontation with Pharaoh. Odd, isn't it? Moses is more afraid of how the conversation with Pharaoh will go, rather than how questioning God will be received. Over the next forty years, Moses learns to rely on the Lord and trust in Him. Moses will have forty more years of practice learning to have faith in God. But right now, on this mountain, Moses is still learning that trust.

---

12. I know I said I wouldn't use other scripture as commentary, but allow me a few exceptions. Matthew 19:26 says, "But Jesus looked at them and said, For mortals it is impossible, but for God all things are possible."

God Assigns a Spokesman

After Moses expresses concern about his public speaking skills, God replies,

> Who hath made man's mouth? or who maketh the dumb, or deaf, or the seeing, or the blind? have not I the Lord?
>
> Now therefore go, and I will be with thy mouth, and teach thee what thou shalt say.
>
> And he said, O my Lord, send, I pray thee, by the hand of him whom thou wilt send.
>
> And the anger of the Lord was kindled against Moses, and he said, Is not Aaron the Levite thy brother? I know that he can speak well. And also, behold, he cometh forth to meet thee: and when he seeth thee, he will be glad in his heart.
>
> And thou shalt speak unto him, and put words in his mouth: and I will be with thy amouth, and with his mouth, and will teach you what ye shall do.
>
> And he shall be thy spokesman unto the people: and he shall be, even he shall be to thee instead of a mouth, and thou shalt be to him instead of God.
>
> And thou shalt take this rod in thine hand, wherewith thou shalt do signs. (KJV, Exodus 4:11–17)

God provides an assistant, a helper, a brother for Moses. Aaron will serve as a spokesperson for Moses.

Aaron

Aaron is the consummate priest. Although the Levitical Priesthood has yet to be established in the story, Aaron is always in that role. He's the one who stands as a representative of God. Aaron is the servant leader, the go-between. In his first assignment, he stands as the mouthpiece of Moses.

God's description of Aaron's role as a spokesperson and prophet is one of the clearest in scripture: "And he himself shall be as a mouth for you, and you shall be to him as God" (Exodus 4:16). Aaron will serve as the spokesperson, doing precisely what Moses tells him. Moses is to say what God tells him. So, God speaks to Moses, Moses to Aaron, and Aaron to the rest in a kind of spiritual daisy-chain. Aaron's the older brother, yet here, he serves and does not lead.

We do not learn of Aaron's life before he became a spokesman. Later we meet his sons and realize he must have had a rich family life. Jewish tradition holds that he was a great leader and peacemaker of the Israelites while in Egypt.[13] Suddenly, he enters the scene and is happy to follow his younger brother. Aaron speaks for Moses, who speaks for God.

Brothers

The story of brothers has been a difficult one in the Bible. The younger brother has been favored, which is the opposite of what the culture would expect. Cain and Abel, Ishmael and Isaac, Esau and Jacob, Joseph and, well, all his brothers—each story doesn't end well. Cain kills Abel. Ishmael and Isaac have to separate. Esau and Jacob eventually reconcile, but at one point, there is the threat of death. Joseph is sold into slavery by his brothers. So, when God gives Moses his older brother, Aaron, as a spokesperson, we'd be right to be a little hesitant. Here is where Aaron shines.

Aaron supports Moses. Content to be number two, Aaron will wait at the bottom of Sinai. He'll accompany Moses to speak from him in the courts of Pharaoh. Even though he is older, he will serve.

Aaron and Moses Reunited

The name *Aaron* means "bright" or "to become light."[14] It also sounds similar to the word that we use for mount or hill. Embedded in his name is an example, which can be seen above the world,

---

13. Rabbi Hillel used to say, "Be one of the disciples of Aaron, loving peace and pursuing peace" (m. *Avot* 1:12).
14. F. Brown, S. Driver, and C. Briggs, *The Brown-Driver-Briggs Hebrew and English Lexicon* (Boston: Hendrickson Publishers, 2004), 215 and 2022. See also entry 5094.

solid and steadfast. Aaron is like a "city set on a hill that cannot be hidden" (Matthew 5:14). He is the light that can give us guidance and direction from afar. He is steadfast and immovable. In our first encounter with Aaron, these characteristics are perfectly exemplified.

After Moses sees God on Sinai, Aaron and Moses reunite, seemingly after forty years. Moses returns to Midian, to his family. That's when we hear about Aaron: "And the Lord said to Aaron, 'Go to the wilderness to meet Moses.' So he went and met him on the mountain of God, and kissed him" (NRSV, Exodus 4:27).

God calls, and Aaron goes. He just *follows* God's commands. His greeting of Moses is sublime. He kisses him. When some would be jealous or spiteful, Aaron shows humility and love. In a kiss, he embraces his younger brother in peace and unity. Like Joseph and Hyrum, or Mary and Martha, the love between siblings is joyous and heartwarming, while rare in scripture. Where Aaron could be resentful or want the power, he shows love.

> So Moses told Aaron all the words of the Lord who had sent him, and all the signs which He had commanded him. Then Moses and Aaron went and gathered together all the elders of the children of Israel. And Aaron spoke all the words which the Lord had spoken to Moses. Then he did the signs in the sight of the people. So the people believed; and when they heard that the Lord had visited the children of Israel and that He had looked on their affliction, then they bowed their heads and worshiped. (Exodus 4:28–31)

Aaron becomes the support, the brother, the partner to Moses. He is a mountain, a pillar of strength, and Moses tells him the whole story. Aaron shares the miracles and the wonders, and the Israelites believe. In the following chapters, we see Aaron telling Pharaoh God's words. He is brave in becoming a voice of freedom for his people. He tells Pharaoh, "Let my people go." He believes in the Lord. He has faith, and he trusts the words Moses and the Lord tell him. What he's doing is right, and he can save a nation. Over and over again, Aaron repeats the Lord's words with faith.

Aaron is like a mountain, a firm support. In Hebrew, the idea of a mountain is not just tall and stately. It is something gathered in. Aaron reminds us that he is gathering Israel. His firm faith and support of the prophet lead the people to salvation.

The Exodus

You've probably read the story. Maybe you have seen the movie or watched the musical. Pharaoh continues to oppress the Israelites. They have grown even more extensive, more populous, but Pharaoh's oppression has reached a fevered pitch. Moses, now in Midian, is called of God. On a mountain called Sinai, Moses hears the Lord from a burning bush.

The Lord tells Moses, "I know their sufferings, and I have come down to deliver them from the Egyptians, and to bring them up out of that land to a good and broad land, a land flowing with milk and honey" (NRSV, Exodus 3:7–8). But freedom from oppression isn't the Lord's only goal. Instead, He wants to meet with them, as He did with Moses. The Lord continues, "I will be with you . . . when you have brought the people out of Egypt, you shall worship God on this mountain" (NRSV, Exodus 3:12). God wants to free the Israelites from tyranny and slavery. He also wants them to know Him and enter once again into His presence.

First, the Lord meets with Moses. On Sinai, He calls to Moses from a bush. There, on a mountain, He invites Moses, and us, to know Him.

Plagues, Passover, and the Sea

The Israelites, including Moses, Miriam, and Aaron, await deliverance and salvation from the oppression of Pharaoh. We know the story. Moses, accompanied by Aaron as spokesman, tells Pharaoh, "Let my people go!" He asks Pharaoh over and over. Yet, Pharaoh's heart is hard, and he will not relent. In a series of nine plagues, God shows His power to Pharaoh. But Pharaoh does nothing. He does not let the Israelites go to worship God. Finally, the last terrible plague, the death of the firstborn, comes. The Hebrews paint the blood of an unblemished male lamb on their doors so that the Lord will pass over them. They eat the sacrifice, standing, dressed for a quick departure. The Passover, with its celebration of salvation and sacrifice, begins. The firstborn children of Egypt die. Pharaoh and his people suffer the fate they inflicted on the Israelites. Pharaoh orders the death of the Israelite boys, and his evil is visited back on him and his people. Finally, Pharaoh lets them leave. All of Israel departs.

In a fit of rage, Pharaoh changes his mind. Gathering up his army and his chariots, he pursues the Israelites to the banks of the sea. All the people of Israel, led by God, find themselves backed into a trap. On one side, the mighty Pharaoh, the superpower of the ancient world armed with chariots and horses, drives the Israelites. Their backs are to the sea. There is no escape. Trapped, only a miracle can save them.

Back to the Sea

We find ourselves in the story of Exodus trapped between the churning chaos of the sea and the evil power of Egypt and its army. The only place we can turn is to God.

"But Moses said to the people, 'Do not be afraid. Stand still, and see the salvation of the Lord, which He will accomplish for you today; . . . for the Lord will fight for you'" (NRSV, Exodus 14:13–14).

God performs a miracle.

> Then Moses stretched out his hand over the sea; and the Lord caused the sea to go back by a strong east wind all that night, and made the sea into dry land, and the waters were divided. So the children of Israel went into the midst of the sea on the dry ground, and the waters were a wall to them on their right and on their left. (NRSV, Exodus 14:21–22)

The sea parts, as God causes the sea to pile up on each side, and the children of Israel walk through on dry land. They are saved—miraculously delivered from Pharaoh and his army! At the moment, when Moses leads the Israelites through the sea, Miriam re-enters the story. She rejoins Moses as they both sing a song. On the other side of the Red Sea, after the water crash is over, the Egyptians and the children of Israel are saved. Moses sings a song. This is perhaps the very first song in scripture that we hear. Moses and Aaron have confronted Pharaoh in the name of the Lord. After the plagues and wonders, they escape slavery. Miriam rejoins the narrative precisely at this moment.

Miriam as Prophetess

Miriam is the first woman bestowed with the title *prophetess*. We often think that that role is reserved for men called from the holy priesthood. While that is common, the gift of prophecy is not given only to men but to all of God's children. Perhaps it is a little rarer than some of the other gifts of the Spirit, yet here in one of the opening books of the Old Testament, we find a woman bestowed with this great gift of God (see 1 Corinthians 12; Moroni 10; D&C 46). Under the direction of the keys of the priesthood, Miriam is given this wondrous gift of the Spirit. Moses, Aaron, and Miriam all lead the people with this gift. We learn of Miriam's great spiritual gift, this role that blesses her people after crossing the Red Sea.[15]

Chapter, Verse, and Poems

Scriptural scholars have often noted the different types of genre and writing used by the prophets and scribes who create scripture. We're most familiar with narratives, which help us understand the

---

15. While most scholars now think it is reed sea or Sea of Reeds, I am going to hold to the Red Sea or the sea. Red Sea is a mistranslation of the term *Yam Suf* (Sea of Reeds).

overarching themes that we can relate to our own lives. That is the most popular form of writing in scripture. But another form called poetry is also very popular. Our King James Version of the Bible in English has been formatted in chapters and verses. The ancient scripture writers, however, did not use this format. Those were created later by Stephen Langton, Archbishop of Canterbury, around 1227 C.E.[16] Langton put in our modern chapter and verse breaks, making it easier to find and reference scriptures. Langton had to decide each chapter and verse, carefully following the stories and breaking them into understandable sections. As a result, everything looks the same, whether poetry or narrative, quotes or conversation—chapters and verses. Of course, Hebrew authors did not write with the same grammatical structure we have today. There were no paragraphs or commas. Frankly, there was no punctuation. Everything just looked like a giant run-on sentence.

Now, we use punctuation to break up sentences and paragraphs, helping give clarity and meaning. One thing modern English authors do is write poems and songs in verse. If you're reading your scriptures, you will notice there isn't much verse in the KJV. Other translations help us out and "poemify" songs to help us see when they are happening. (I just made up that word. Feel free to use it).

The Song of the Sea is just like that—hard to notice because of the chapter and verse notation. But it is a song!

Why a Song?

Why use a song at all? Poetry and songs help us understand the emotion of an event. They tie us into something powerful that sometimes is hard to express. Spiritual things like miracles, prayer, hopes and prophecies, even laments and despair are often expressed in verse and poetry. I like to think we do the same thing today. We

---

16. O. Schmidt, Über verschiedene Eintheilungen der heiligen Schrift (Graz, 1892) and A. Landgraf, 'Die Schriftzitate in der Scholastik um die Wende des 12. zum 13. Jahrh.', Bib., xviii (1937), 74–94.

do it in a song to say something powerful, a strong emotion, or a profound event. Whether in a hymn or a popular ballad, we tell our feelings and spiritual interactions through verse. Emotions are hard to express in just words. In a poem, or even better, a song, we can feel the emotion. A song immediately conveys much more than most words alone. It's no different in the Bible.

Dancing is taking up another emotional notch. When songs are not enough to contain the emotion, a person dances. If text is regular emotion, then poetry is next level, and the most extreme expression is dance. Miriam and the Israelites will dance and sing on the banks of the sea. After being slaves for so long, having their children murdered, and then being followed across the desert by Pharaoh, there is undoubtedly a lot of fear. The events of the Exodus are full of emotion. The plagues and then the miracle of the Passover are astounding. Then, led by the Lord as a cloud by day and a pillar of fire by night, they see miracles each day. Finally, crossing the sea on the dry ground is a cause for relief, joy, and astonishment. Then, having crossed the sea on dry land, saved by the Lord, there is an excess of emotion. This is when they sing and dance.

The Song of the Sea: Brother and Sister Celebrate

On the banks of the Red Sea, after the Egyptians are defeated, Moses and Miriam sing. Moses sings the first song of the Old Testament called The Song of the Sea (see Exodus 15:1–18). After Moses sings, Miriam takes a timbrel, like a tambourine, and leads the people singing and dancing.

> Sing to the Lord
> For He is highly exalted
> Both horse and rider
> He has thrown into the sea

The Song of the Sea is a devotional. It praises God for victory and salvation. It is an emotional response to a harrowing and miraculous event. Moses sings of the Lord protecting them. We can imagine the fear as Pharaoh's army and chariots are chasing them down. We feel the relief as the Israelites escape through the sea. Remember this song. Remember that Miriam leads the people in a song about God overcoming, salvation, and celebration of a deliverance long-awaited. A song of victory and salvation will come up again about the Savior.

The Song of the Sea, also known as Moses's song, as we see in Exodus 15 and sung by Moses and Miriam, is still practiced today. Some Jewish faiths sing part of this or pray part of this every morning as part of their rituals.[17] In Jewish tradition, this song will be sung again in the world to come. Eastern Orthodox, Roman Catholic, and other Christian faith traditions use these verses as part of their Easter services. Using this song in morning prayers, the High Holidays, and Easter reminds us of deliverance, both in the past and one to come.

This song of Moses is sometimes even referred to as the Song of Moses and Miriam in some English translations of the Bible. I love the reference to these great heroes and their work as prophets as they sing out a song of salvation and deliverance.

Reread the Song of the Sea

Take a moment and go to Exodus 15. Read this compelling song—this great song of victory and praise to God. Imagine yourself on the banks of the Red Sea, relief washing over you as you realize you have been saved and delivered from evil hands. And what's left but to cry out to God in praise and song. To dance and sing, with joy and tears, they show their overwhelming emotion. This is the song of Miriam.

We can feel the same emotion, the same victory, when God delivers us. We can feel the joy of escaping after we have no way

---

17. https://www.jewishvirtuallibrary.org/the-daily-services-of-jewish-prayers
Also see, *Sechant*, https://www.sefaria.org/Siddur_Ashkenaz%2C_
Weekday%2C_Shacharit%2C_Preparatory_Prayers%2C_Asher_
Yatzar?lang=bi

out. When we are trapped by evil, we can sing out our relief at our unexpected liberation. When we are cornered by sin, the Lord alone can deliver us. That is the message of the Song of the Sea.

Remember Moses, who wanted so desperately to save an Israelite from an Egyptian taskmaster? Moses has delivered more than one Israelite. With the power of God, he has delivered every single one. What about Aaron? He faced down Pharaoh and his magicians face to face. And Miriam, the girl who placed a boy in an ark? She leads the people through the sea to new life. The three are deliverers of Israel.

"I will sing to the LORD, for he has triumphed gloriously;
    horse and rider he has thrown into the sea.
The LORD is my strength and my might,[a]
    and he has become my salvation;
this is my God, and I will praise him,
    my father's God, and I will exalt him.
The LORD is a warrior;
    the Lord is his name.

"Pharaoh's chariots and his army he cast into the sea;
    his picked officers were sunk in the Red Sea.[b]
The floods covered them;
    they went down into the depths like a stone.
Your right hand, O LORD, glorious in power—
    your right hand, O Lord, shattered the enemy.
In the greatness of your majesty you overthrew your adversaries;
    you sent out your fury, it consumed them like stubble.
At the blast of your nostrils the waters piled up,
    the floods stood up in a heap;
    the deeps congealed in the heart of the sea.
The enemy said, 'I will pursue, I will overtake,
    I will divide the spoil, my desire shall have its fill of them.
    I will draw my sword, my hand shall destroy them.'
You blew with your wind, the sea covered them;
    they sank like lead in the mighty waters.

"Who is like you, O LORD, among the gods?
    Who is like you, majestic in holiness,
    awesome in splendor, doing wonders?

You stretched out your right hand,
 the earth swallowed them.

"In your steadfast love you led the people whom you redeemed;
 you guided them by your strength to your holy abode.
The peoples heard, they trembled;
 pangs seized the inhabitants of Philistia.
Then the chiefs of Edom were dismayed;
 trembling seized the leaders of Moab;
 all the inhabitants of Canaan melted away.
Terror and dread fell upon them;
 by the might of your arm, they became still as a stone
until your people, O Lord, passed by,
 until the people whom you acquired passed by.
You brought them in and planted them on the mountain of your
 own possession,
 the place, O Lord, that you made your abode,
 the sanctuary, O Lord, that your hands have established.
The Lord will reign forever and ever." (NRSV, Exodus 15:1–18)

Miriam, the Name

Miriam has grown up. She is no longer the little girl at the Nile but a prophet. What else do we know about her? Miriam's name is unclear in its meaning. It may mean many things. The Hebrew root *mrr* means bitter, perhaps reminding us of the bitterness of bondage.[18] We see a similar noun in Hebrew coming from the same Hebrew root *myrrh*, the gift given to Christ after His birth by the Magi. The kingly gift of bitter myrrh reminds us of death and sin that only the Savior can only overcome.

Additionally, the name Miriam reminds us of all the many lessons that we only learn through bitter experience. Another meaning from the verse in Isaiah 40:14 (and made famous in the movie *Chariots of Fire*) is "the nations are as a drop of water in a bucket."

---

18. F. Brown, S. Driver, and C. Briggs, *The Brown-Driver-Briggs Hebrew and English Lexicon* (Boston: Hendrickson Publishers, 2004), 4751, 4843.

Miriam has a lot of water connotations, from saving Moses from the Nile to crossing the sea and dancing in prophecy. Later, as the Israelites wander in the desert, a miraculous well is named Well of Miriam, giving life and water throughout their wanderings (see Exodus 15:20–21).[19] Finally, the Hebrew root *mry* or *meri* means rebellion. The rebellion against Pharaoh and perhaps Moses—but we're coming to that.

Miriam, the prophetess, has a name with more than one meaning, much like her complexity. She is born in bitterness and rebels. She is a savior, like water, both of the Nile and the sea the Israelites crossed. She is the life-giving water of a well, as the prophecy of God, giving life to all. There is another story of Miriam, one in which she fails and is chastised. Aaron and Moses also have additional failures. But first, let's return to the holy mountain.

God's Covenant Promises

So far, we have learned about each of the siblings in Moses's family. Moses was miraculously saved as a baby from a terrible Pharaoh and an Israelite raised in the Egyptian court. We also learned his protector was his older sister, Miriam, who was led by God to guard the ark. Then, we were introduced to Aaron, the stalwart supporter and spokesperson for Moses. There are more stories to tell, more insights to these wondrously real and flawed humans that God loved—and are so much like us. Before we continue, there is a highlight to the book of Exodus. If we miss this critical story, we will miss the key ideas of the law.

The story of the Exodus is one of the foundational stories of all of scripture. It is a story of God's blessing. It reminds us of His love and deliverance. It also reminds us that God keeps His covenant promises. In the pages of Exodus, we see the birth of a nation when Israel itself truly comes into being. We see the references repeatedly to how it is the culmination of the promised blessing of Abraham's

---

19. https://ohr.edu/explore_judaism/ask_the_rabbi/ask_the_rabbi/7033

covenant. Do you remember the covenant of Abraham? God promises that the great patriarch Abraham and matriarch Sarah, their posterity, their offspring, and their family will be as great as the sands of the sea and the stars in the sky. The book of Exodus starts with that exact reference that the Israelites as inheritors of the covenant have become numerous. "The Israelites were fruitful and multiplied; they multiplied and grew exceedingly strong, so that the land was filled with them" (NRSV, Exodus 1:5).

The Lord has blessed the children of Abraham. God has been with them, keeping His covenant promises. The story of the Exodus also shows the covenant promises of a land, a special promised place where Abraham's family can live and grow and thrive. Exodus is leading out of Egypt and hinting at that place they'll discover. It won't happen in Exodus but a few books later, when we reach Canaan, the promised land. What we know today as Israel is evidence of God keeping His promises, first to Abraham and then to all of us. There are more covenants the Lord makes with people. God makes them with the Israelites on Sinai.

In Exodus, we meet God on a mountain, a unique place where Moses meets and speaks with the Lord. More than just talking, we see connection, communion, and understanding. "The Lord used to speak to Moses face to face, as one speaks to a friend" (NRSV, Exodus 33:11). Like Moses, we have an invitation back to His presence. We can return to Eden, be the image bearing humanity He always intended. We can speak to the Lord face to face. We can be His disciple, child, and friend.

What is the most significant part of the story of the Exodus? Is it the ten plagues of Egypt? The Passover when God protected the firstborn? Is it the miracle of crossing the Red Sea and the Israelites walking through on dry ground? All of those are amazing, miraculous events. The most important part, the highlight, and the culmination of everything is in Exodus 19. (I can almost hear you flipping pages to find out what is in Exodus 19. Go ahead, find out. I'll be here when you get back).

PART III: THE LAWGIVER

The Most Important Part of the Exodus

The most important part of the Exodus story is the Lord's invitation to become a holy nation, a peculiar people, a kingdom of priests and priestesses. The Lord invites us back into His presence to be His friends. He tells us exactly how we are to do it. We are to become holy. We enter into a covenant, a new invitation to become God's special people. God invites Moses, then all the Israelites, and finally all of us, to the mountain. The Lord extends to all of us the invitation to meet Him. That is the crux of the story of Exodus—how we were delivered out of this world and invited into a higher, newer, more spiritual plane. God invites us to return to Eden. We, like the children of Israel, can be welcomed into the presence of God.

> Thus you shall say to the house of Jacob, and tell the children of Israel, "You have seen what I did to the Egyptians, and how I bore you on eagles' wings and brought you to Myself. Now therefore, if you will indeed obey My voice and keep My covenant, then you shall be a special treasure to Me above all people; for all the earth is Mine. And you shall be to Me a kingdom of priests and a holy nation." (NRSV, Exodus 19:3–6)

We are each Moses, Miriam, and Aaron. We are each the Israelites, given a choice to serve God or Pharaoh. God invites each of us to meet Him face to face.

Is the story over once we meet God on a mountain-temple? In this story, and ours, the next phase is just beginning. Now we have to learn how to become a covenant people.

Rebellion in the Desert

After Moses returns to Sinai to receive the law, things do not go perfectly. Moses has been up there for a long time. The Israelites become concerned. They start to doubt and worry. Moses is taking too long, and something must have happened to him! They go to Aaron and ask him to make them an idol to represent the Lord. Wait, what? Let's recap.

The Israelites were under bondage and servitude to Egypt for hundreds of years. After witnessing the plagues, the Passover, and the crossing of the sea, they arrive at Mount Sinai. There they witness the power of the Lord in lightning and thundering. They see God work on their behalf. Now, while Moses receives the law, they are down below. And they doubt. They go back to what they knew in Egypt.

Exodus 32 does not paint a flattering picture. They seem like backsliders, uncommitted, or weak. God just saved them! He just delivered them. How can they forget so quickly? The sad truth is, they are us. As hard as it is to admit it, we can, at times, be precisely the same. Sure, there are moments of great faith and profound obedience. I wonder if we don't tell those stories of incredible faith because they are unique and rare. It is far more common for us to doubt, backslide, and misunderstand.

There is good news. The Lord has a plan for the Israelites. He has a plan for us. The Lord is not surprised. Let's see what happens.

The Golden Calf

When the people saw that Moses delayed to come down from the mountain, the people gathered around Aaron, and said to him, "Come, make gods for us, who shall go before us; as for this Moses, the man who brought us up out of the land of Egypt, we do not know what has become of him." (NRSV, Exodus 32:1)

The people worry. They doubt. They still do not know or trust Moses. The ringleaders are worse, and they do not follow the Lord. They abandon God and plot to take others along with them in their evil.

Aaron said to them, "Take off the gold rings that are on the ears of your wives, your sons, and your daughters, and bring them to me." So all the people took off the gold rings from their ears, and brought them to Aaron. He took the gold from them, formed it in a mold, and cast an image of a calf; and they said, "These are your gods, O Israel, who brought you up out of the land of Egypt!" When Aaron saw this, he built an altar before it; and Aaron made proclamation and said, "Tomorrow shall be a festival to the Lord." They rose early the next day, and offered burnt offerings and brought sacrifices of well-being; and the people sat down to eat and drink, and rose up to revel. (NRSV, Exodus 32:2–6)

Aaron Makes a Golden Calf

Here's where the story takes an odd turn. Aaron, this important priest, this brother of Moses who has helped the Israelites overcome Pharaoh, makes an idol. He gathers up the Israelites' golden earrings and ornaments, and constructs a calf. He tells the people the calf is the Lord. The people throw a party, and it gets out of control.

Moses, still on Sinai, gets a report from the Lord. "Go down at once! Your people, whom you brought up out of the land of Egypt, have acted perversely; they have been quick to turn aside from the way that I commanded them" (NRSV, Exodus 32:7–8).

When Moses gets there, he is angry and disappointed at what the people have done. They've just witnessed all these great things. How did this happen? This is where we scratch our heads a little and try to understand what each person is thinking. What about Aaron? Why did Aaron do this? We'll never really know exactly what motivated Aaron. Some scholars believe he was stalling for time. Or perhaps it is important that he didn't create an idol for *other* gods. Or, maybe he is not to blame, as the people do what they want. There is no talk of Miriam either during this time. We just don't know why Aaron did such a thing.

Scripture pushes us to examine and ponder. We have to see ourselves in the story, in the results, and come to our own conclusions. Aaron wasn't punished, so perhaps there is something else to this story we do not know. We do know one thing: The Levites, the tribe that Moses, Aaron, and Miriam belong to, did not worship the golden calf. Moses stands and says, "'Who's on the Lord's side? Come to me!' and all of the sons of Levi gathered around him" (NRSV, Exodus 32:26). The tribe of Levi stays true. And they go, and they take care of the issue.

The Attributes of the Lord

Shortly after the event of the golden calf, we learn something about the Lord. In one of the most quoted scriptures of the entire Old Testament, God tells us about Himself. In the middle of revealing the law, He shares His characteristics and attributes.

> The Lord descended in the cloud and stood with him there, and proclaimed the name, "The Lord." The Lord passed before him, and proclaimed, "The Lord, the Lord, a God merciful and gracious, slow to anger, and abounding in steadfast love and faithfulness, keeping steadfast love for the thousandth generation." (NRSV, Exodus 36:5–7)

The Lord tells us about Himself in His own words. He tells us He is merciful. He is gracious. He keeps His covenant promises and will always do so. His love is so great that He will love our families and us forever. Despite our failings, our doubts, even our disobedience, He is still our God. When we stumble, consider making golden calves, or forget the miracles He has done, He will be merciful.

The God of Moses, Miriam, and Aaron is a God of love. Our God is faithful and loving.

Holding up the Hands That Droop

After the golden calf incident, we may wonder if Aaron stayed true. What do we make of Aaron? There is one story that helps answer the question.

As the Israelites approach Rephidim on their long march in the desert, they are attacked by the nation of Amalek. Moses has Joshua choose men to go into battle to defend the Israelites. Moses, Aaron, and Hur climb a nearby hill, and they see a miracle. Whenever Moses raises his hands, the Israelites begin to win. Moses's arms start to tire and fall to his sides. Aaron, ever the supporter, holds Moses's arms up. Aaron and Hur each grab an arm and hold Moses up so the Israelites can win (see Exodus 17:13).

Aaron is ever faithful to the prophet. He figuratively and literally supports Moses. Aaron, the older brother and high priest, holds his brother's arms. What a powerful message for us today. When the prophet commands, we can support him or choose another path. Ultimately, Moses helps the Israelites win, just as God's mouthpiece does for us today. He guides and leads us. Will you support him?

Lessons from Aaron

At times the Lord needs all of us to be the follower. We can learn to serve and to obey. The Israelites were servants in Egypt. When they escaped, they became the servants of the Lord. Aaron was a perfect leader, teaching them and loving them as they grew up. We each have the choice to learn to follow and serve before we can lead. In God's kingdom, a servant is a noble calling.

How many times are we asked to take the back seat? Maybe we are not given the calling that we thought we deserved. We don't get the big promotion at work. We don't do as well at school. We're not the prominent athlete. We're just average. And yet, that's the heroism of Aaron. Through all these great and miraculous events, Aaron serves. We have a choice to be "brilliant at the basics"—to serve and obey as Aaron did.

In the Wilderness

The fourth book of the law is called "In the Wilderness." At least, that's its Hebrew name, which I think is much more descriptive of what happens. We call it Numbers because it starts and ends with a census. And while the census has some interesting theological insights, the idea of struggle being a wilderness is an apt name for the events in its pages. Things don't go that well after the Exodus and covenant with God on Sinai. The Israelites struggle, wander, and learn to follow God in their spiritual and desert wilderness.

God invites the Israelites to the holy mountain. He gives them covenants and instructions, and before Moses has even descended, they fail. While Moses is up on the mountain, the people despair and make a golden calf idol. It is shocking how quickly we—ahem, I mean "they—forget their covenants. Despite these failures, the Lord continues to work with them. God leads them on their journey in the wilderness. It is telling that after making covenants, things are not perfect. Our lives don't suddenly become easy. Being a covenant bearer doesn't miraculously make our life simple. Instead, like the Israelites, our covenants bind us to the Lord so that our lives can be blessed, despite our challenges.

In the wilderness, we see more failures and disappointments. Our heroes struggle. We will only cover a couple of examples. But if you watch closely, you'll see how God continues to work with them. Despite their sins, God uses their mistakes to make them into something better, the humanity He knew they could be. The book of Numbers, if we aren't careful, can look like a bunch of mistakes. It would be too easy to look down on the Israelites and shake our heads in astonishment at how quickly they forget the miracles they have witnessed. Sadly, I think "In the Wilderness" might strike a little too close to home. I think we are all a little Israelite, wandering in the desert, failing, and forgetting. There is hope. There are some lessons to be learned—lessons we can each realize in our wanderings in life.

Aaron and Moses at Meribah

As the people begin their wanderings, they lack essential resources. One of the first is water. The Lord repeatedly provides water for the Israelites. They are fresh out of Egypt and can only find bitter water. The Lord instructs Moses to throw a bitter tree branch into the water, and it is miraculously made drinkable (see Exodus 15:22). Not long after, the Israelites run out of water again. God commands Moses to strike a rock with his staff, and water gushes out (see Exodus 17:1–7).

Later, after they wander for nearly forty years, they once again complain about water. They come to a place called Meribah and need water. This time the people complain to Moses and Aaron (Miriam has recently died). The brothers consult the Lord and are told to gather the community and speak to the rock, and water will come out. Moses and Aaron gather the people around the rock. Moses chastises the people and calls them rebels. Instead of speaking to the rock as commanded, he strikes the rock twice with Aaron's staff (see Numbers 20).

It is an odd story. Scholars call things "enigmatic" when we would just use the words *puzzling* or *strange*. There are theories that Miriam was somehow related to the well, and her death is upsetting. Or perhaps the stories of wells and rocks are one big story. We just don't know that much about the story. What we do know is the results. Because of the events, neither Moses or Aaron can enter the promised land.

Aaron as High Priest

Aaron is a brave man with flaws. He is involved in the creation of the golden calf, and now he is guilty at Meribah.

Aaron is a priest. He is the high priest, so these stories of failure are more pronounced. Now, we may look at this and say that Aaron failed through all of this. If Aaron had just been more faithful, and if he had persevered to the end, he would have been allowed into the promised land. I choose to look at the story of Aaron a little differently. Aaron is like all of us. Aaron is a flawed, imperfect human. His sins, from rebellion to doubts, are the same that we have. Only the Lord, only Jesus Christ, can truly lead us into the promised land. We follow the Savior because He will be the one, the perfect human that's going to lead us onward. I love the example of Aaron (and Moses and Miriam) because we are much more like them than we are the Lord. Aaron teaches us about the way, the covenant path we can follow.

Aaron, a Tribute

Aaron is given his prophetic gifts. His sole calling in life is not to follow Moses around. Later we see his family having special duties as priests. Aaron serves as high priest. He's referred to as one of the ancestors of John the Baptist. He's a representative of virtue and obedience, despite his few failings.

While the whole tribe (Moses and Miriam's same tribe of Levi) is assigned the priesthood, Aaron's family serves as high priest. Like the role of spokesperson, the priests represent all of Israel in the tabernacle and later the temple. We honor Aaron by calling the priesthood the Aaronic Priesthood.

There is a series of psalms called the "Song of Ascents," comprising Psalms 120–134. Traditionally, pilgrims would sing each of the psalms ascending the hills leading to Jerusalem. There are also steps leading into the temple, and some would sing one psalm for each step. Psalm 133 beautifully references Aaron:

> How good and pleasant it is
>   when God's people live together in unity!
> It is like precious oil poured on the head,
>   running down on the beard,
> running down on Aaron's beard,
>   down on the collar of his robe.
> It is as if the dew of Hermon
>   were falling on Mount Zion.
> For there the Lord bestows his blessing,
>   even life forevermore.

Aaron is a peacemaker, a bringer of life and joy. At the end of his life, we learn what great love the people have for him. The people mourn when Aaron dies at age 123. One hundred and twenty-three years is a long life, so why did the people grieve? They loved him like their own close family member. The scriptures say the entire people mourn thirty days, the customary period of mourning for an immediately family member. Aaron, their high priest, is a brother, father, and family member to each of them. Their beloved Aaron is gone.

What a fitting tribute to the man who delivered them.

And what of Miriam? How does her story end?

Miriam's Exile

Miriam's story starts with her saving her brother. She leads the Israelites in song. She is called a prophetess. She is a beautiful example, yet there is one story of failure. Because of her actions, she is banished outside of the camp.

Miriam's Mistakes

As prophetess, Miriam is referred to again in the book of Numbers. At this point, the children of Israel have left Mount Sinai and learn while wandering in the wilderness. They have many rebellions and many trials. The whole of Israel is tested, and Miriam is no different. They are learning to become the people of God. They have committed to being like Him but have a long way to go. As a covenant people, the children of Israel are a little bit like us. They struggle as they learn. They push boundaries, and they learn what to do and what not to do.

We have already left Mount Sinai in the story. Miriam, and the children of Israel in Exodus 19, have taken part of the Mosaic covenant. They become a covenant people to follow the Lord. And now they're practicing. They are learning how to be a people who follow the Lord. They are learning how to listen to God and become holy. Miriam is learning, too.

While they are wandering, they have trials. They run out of bread, and they receive manna. They run out of food, and they are given quail. They also run out of water. Moses strikes a rock and water comes out. It follows them throughout their journeys and is called the Well of Miriam (see 1 Corinthians 10:4; Exodus

15:20–21). They are blessed so their clothes and shoes do not wear out. The Lord leads them and provides for them in the wilderness.

Remember, Miriam is a prophetess. She has felt the Lord speak to her and through her. In music and dance, she has shared the revelations of the Lord. Aaron, too, is a prophet, receiving revelations and guidance from God. He will become high priest, while Moses is the prophet and the leader.

Miriam's Rebellion

There is a confusing and kind of embarrassing story about Miriam. At this point, they've been wandering the desert. Moses has a wife named Zipporah. Miriam starts to complain about Moses's wife. We're unsure what the complaint is. It may be that she is from a country outside of Israel. She's from Cush, which was culturally different from the Israelites. It could be a case of racism. Alternatively, some scholars believe that Miriam was speaking up *on behalf* of Moses's wife. Moses had taken a vow that required him to stay away from his wife. Miriam, in turn, was complaining about Moses being apart from his wife. Either way, Miriam begins by complaining about Moses, and it starts with his wife.

Now, something rebellious happens. Miriam escalates the issue and gets Aaron involved. She says, "Has the Lord spoken only through Moses? Has he not spoken through us also?" (Numbers 12:2). The complaining ends ominously. "And the Lord heard it" (Numbers 12:2).

The Lord calls all three siblings to meet with Him immediately. There, in front of the Tent of Meeting, the Lord descends and says,

When there are prophets among you,
I the Lord make myself known to them in visions;
I speak to them in dreams.
Not so with my servant Moses;
he is entrusted with all my house.
With him I speak face to face— clearly, not in riddles;
and he beholds the form of the Lord. (NRSV, Numbers 12:6–8)

Miriam speaks out against Moses. We see her stumble, and at this point, the Lord steps in. He descends on the tabernacle and calls the three siblings together. He asks about their behavior. Here is something remarkable. The Lord recognizes that Miriam and Aaron have both been prophetic. They have both felt the Spirit of the Lord and have spoken for Him. There's a lesson in here for us. The Lord desires all of us to hear Him. In just one chapter earlier, this is clearly stated.

All the Lord's People Were Prophets

This is important, so let's pause here for a second. Miriam and Aaron have both been prophets. Not only that, but God desires for all of us to hear Him. In Numbers 11, a bit of stir is created when two men other men, Eldad and Medad, prophesy. Joshua, Moses's assistant and future leader of the Israelites, runs to tell Moses.

"My lord, Moses, stop them!"

But Moses said, "Are you jealous for my sake? Would that all the Lord's people were prophets and that the Lord would put his spirit on them!" (NRSV, Numbers 11:28–29).

The Lord desires all His people to be prophets, have the gift of revelation, and hear His Spirit. What an exceptional thought. The Lord desires for all His people—*all of us*—to have the gift of revelation.

So, what did Miriam do wrong?

Miriam's Mistake

Miriam sins in two ways. First, she complains about her brother. It is hard in families, and close relationships heighten our emotions. Knowing the details of Moses's marriage may have introduced too much information, too much liberty. She was too close to their private information as husband and wife. But that may not be the only issue.

Miriam complains about Moses's calling. While she has received revelation, she wonders why she doesn't have more authority or honor. In this, she oversteps. And the Lord is evident just how far. The Lord leaves. Aaron looks over, and Miriam is covered in leprosy. Her skin is flaky and dying.

Moses cries out, "Oh Lord, please heal her!" (NRSV, Numbers 12:13).

Leprosy and Uncleanliness

Let's take a moment to talk about leprosy. Leprosy is a sign of corruption and death. It may not be a specific disease that afflicts her. Instead, leprosy is one thing that makes Israelites unclean. Biblical uncleanliness is different than just sinning. In the book of Leviticus (that book you probably skip), we learn about holiness. Holiness is the state that God is in. He is holy, and we are commanded to be holy like Him.

Holiness

Holiness means set apart, consecrated, and unique. God is holy and pure. He is unique and separate. He asks us to be more like Him. "You shall be holy, for I the Lord your God am Holy" (NRSV, Leviticus 19:2). In the covenant on Mount Sinai, God invites us into His presence. We are asked to be a special possession.

> "If you obey my voice and keep my covenant, you shall be my treasured possession out of all the peoples. Indeed, the whole earth is mine, but you shall be for me a priestly kingdom and a holy nation." (NRSV, Exodus 19:5–6)

Being holy is being consecrated and specially set apart to serve the Lord. There are a few things that make us unholy or unclean. These will sound odd, but hang on, and it will make sense and be worth it. The actions that can make a person unholy include touching a dead body, handling any reproductive fluids, or having leprosy. At first glance, nothing is tying these all together. But all of them have to do with life. They are also things that are normal during our day-to-day living. We will occasionally have to bury the dead, come in contact with special bodily fluids, and even become sick. However, contact with reproductive fluids and contact with the dead are events in which death has occurred. These are not examples of new life being created. Thus, they are seen as unholy. God is about life, not corruption. We are at risk when we have experienced these before being in God's presence.

Being unclean is being in the presence of corruption and death. Luckily, in ancient days a person could perform some cleansing, offer a sacrifice, maybe wait a few days, and then be back into a state of holiness.

We can also become unclean. We can offend the Spirit of life and drive the Spirit away. Corruption can be more than just a physical expression in our day. We can repent, partake of the sacrament of the Lord's Supper, and be refreshed and renewed. On the outside of the temple is written, "Holiness to the Lord. The House of the Lord." Like the tabernacle in Moses's day, we go there to be in God's unique presence. We need to be worthy, holy, to enter the place where heaven and earth meet. There the Spirit can flow freely, and we can receive revelation for our own lives. We bind ourselves to the Lord and become "a priestly kingdom and a holy nation."

So, why was Miriam stuck with leprosy?

Miriam had rebelled. In speaking out against the Lord's anointed, she began to be corrupted from within. In Miriam, we see an outward expression of something that had been happening inwardly. Moses cries out for her salvation. She is healed but must retreat outside the camp for seven days.

Exiled

Miriam is exiled, sent out of the camp of Israel. This would have been very serious. They are in the desert, and she is a woman, alone. Imagine what it would have been like. You're in the middle of nowhere. You're unprotected. The closer you are to the center of the camp to the tabernacle, the closer you are to the Lord. So, figuratively, as well as literally, she's the farthest from the Lord. At this point, she's without protection. She's without family and tribe. She's alone in the wilderness.

Her separation is like the separation we all have from the Lord when we sin. Sin removes us from His presence. We become calloused to the Spirit, to His influence, to His guidance. Luckily, the Savior has created a way for us to return. We can repent, calling on His mercy and grace, to come back into the presence of the Lord.

After seven long days, Miriam is welcomed back into the Camp of Israel. Miriam had some failings. The once-great woman has stumbled. Here is where her life resonates for me. Miriam had to come to terms with her failings, her desires, her sin. Like us, when we repent, we have a chance to turn around and change direction if we choose to.

What about the people? Did they turn on Miriam during her time of crisis? During those seven days, the entire Camp of Israel waits. They do not leave. They love their prophetess and welcome her back. What a great message for us. When I sin, I hope that my friends and family will wait for me. I pray they will welcome me back. I know the Lord does. Like the prodigal son, God runs to embrace us and accept us back, placing a ring, robe, and sandals on us.

Miriam's Redemption

If Miriam's story ended here, it might feel like a great tragedy for our hero. Miriam was an incredible woman who had done so much for Israel. She was the one who had helped create the people of God, and yet we leave her banished. Luckily that isn't the end of her story. You see, something miraculous happens, something fantastic and wondrous that teaches us a little bit more about ourselves. The story of Miriam shows us that she was always aligned with Moses. For the rest of her story, she trusts in the Lord. She's always in step and with the prophet. She never speaks out again, never rebels. Her story is Moses's story until her death. She is valiant until the end.

I think we'd like to have spiritual gifts like Miriam. Miriam has excellent gifts, and yet sometimes she stumbles. She may have a little bit of an ego. She may want to follow independently, and she may want to lead instead of just being the follower. Yet, she learns to follow the Lord in all things. She doesn't give up her gift represented beautifully throughout later scriptures.

Miriam, a Tribute

One of the greatest tributes to any person is given to Miriam by the prophet Micah. Centuries after the Exodus, Miriam is still remembered as one of the deliverers of Israel. I love that not just one but all three siblings are praised for what they did to save their people.

"O my people, what have I done to you? . . . For I brought you up from the land of Egypt, and redeemed you from the house of bondage; And I sent before you Moses, Aaron, and Miriam" (NRSV, Micah 6:4).

She is remembered in the Psalms as one who sang the praises of the Lord. It is not just David or Solomon, but Miriam who first prophesied and danced to Him. In the Psalms, we remember that great song of salvation: "Praise him with tambourine and dance; praise him with strings and pipe" (Psalm 150:4).

Her legacy is not just confined to the Old Testament. The New Testament gives tribute to Miriam, too. It can be easy to miss the references because of the language. The Old Testament was written mainly in Hebrew, but the New Testament is in Greek. So, the same names, when translated into their Greek counterparts, don't look the same. Miriam becomes Mary. The New Testament has more than one woman named Mary. Each is a namesake, a tribute to Miriam.

The first Mary we meet is Jesus's mother. When Mary learns she will be the mother of the Savior, what does she do? She sings! She sings a song about the lowly and suffering that will be lifted, elevated, and saved. She, like her namesake, sings of salvation and deliverance. In Luke 14:6–55, the *Magnificat* echoes the joy of Exodus and our hope in Jesus Christ.

Another Mary is like Miriam, too. Mary Magdalene is released from demonic possession. Her diseased condition reminds us of Miriam, stricken with leprosy yet healed by God. Mary Magdalene, like Miriam, is made whole by the Lord.

Mary of Bethany, sister of Martha and Lazarus, is Miriam's namesake and a worthy recipient. She is an ardent supporter of Jesus as the Christ, listening and following the Savior's teachings (see Luke 10:40). It is this Mary who, before Jesus' death, anointed His feet with costly oil and dried them with her hair (see John 11:1–2). Mary is ever faithful. Every Miriam and Mary have prominent roles in the life of Jesus.

They both take leadership positions, supporting Jesus as His disciples and close friends. They have spiritual experiences, right alongside the men, similar to Moses, Aaron, and Miriam.

The Marys of the New Testament live up to their namesake. Heroic, faithful, deliverer, prophetess, calling each of us back to the Lord.

Moses, a Tribute

The legacy of Moses, Miriam, and Aaron continues. Moses, the Deliverer of Israel, is a shining example of faithfulness to the Lord. Moses is "that prophet," the great Deliverer of Israel, the giver of the law, and God's friend. There are few in scripture as written, talked about, quoted, or referred to as Moses. The first five books of the Bible are called "The Books of Moses," showing how much influence he had on the Old Testament, Pearl of Great Price, and the Book of Mormon. Matthew parallels Jesus's life, showing Moses as a symbol of the Great Deliverer. Nephi's journey to the promised land is similar to Moses's. Moses visits the Savior on the Mount of Transfiguration, representing the law and endowing the Lord with the keys of the gathering. He later passes those same keys of the gathering to Joseph Smith. He is the deliverer who assists in gathering us all.

Moses started out trying to defend one Israelite and ended up saving them all. He saved an entire nation and created the Israelites as a people. With the support of his sister, Miriam, and brother, Aaron, Moses changes the course of history.

There is no greater tribute than the Lord's description of Moses. Scripture says, "The Lord would speak to Moses, face to face, as one speaks to a friend" (Exodus 33:11). In His own words, God says, "I am pleased with you, and I know you by name" (Exodus 33:17).

THE JUDGES

The ancient scriptures are not only about successes. Real people with both successes and failures alike cover their pages. One minute we hear of blessings and miracles. Then, we turn the page and read of tragedies, mistakes, and sin. Some stories are cautionary tales, reminding us that the stakes are high in this life. We each have choices to make, and the Lord has taught us how to live a life of righteousness. He has given us our agency. We can choose.

The book of Judges is a cautionary tale. After the Israelites gain the promised land, they struggle. I was kind—they do worse than struggle. They fail. Over and over, they forget the Lord and fall into war, captivity, and sin. It is hard to imagine that after the miracles of the Passover and Exodus, the people have forgotten the Lord. Yet, in the book of Judges, here we are—a story of failings. The last verse of the book sums it up well: "In those days there was no king in Israel; all the people did what was right in their own eyes" (Judges 21:25).

How did they get there? After the Israelites settle into the land of Canaan, they do all right for a bit. After Moses, Joshua leads the people. The Israelites remember their covenants for a while. Joshua dies, and we learn what happened.

"When all that generation had been gathered to their fathers, another generation arose after them who did not know the Lord nor the work which he had done for Israel. Then the children of Israel did evil in the sight of the Lord and served other gods" (NRSV, Judges 2:10–11).

They forgot! They forgot all the miracles and blessings the Lord had given them. How often do we remember all the blessings the Lord has given us? How important is it to remember the Lord's hand in our lives?

The book of Judges tells the story of what happens when we forget the Lord. Putting aside our covenants shows us the result when we take our focus off the Lord.

Why include such tragic stories in scripture? First, they teach us caution. They wave a red flag, pump the brakes, and shout at us to stop. We can read about the series of bad choices, mistakes, and unrepentant sins that lead to tragedy. It is not just one event but a series that leads to real trouble. It reminds us to change, turn around, and repent. The book of Judges reminds us there is still time to change. The tragedies in Judges show us how individuals and an entire people slowly make one bad choice after another. We see how each decision affects the person, how each sin, each moral choice, has consequences.

But there are highlights as well. Deborah leads the people to a great victory. Gideon listens even when he is scared. God continues to love and try and bless the people. Repeatedly, He sends a judge, a leader, who steps in and rescues the people. The judge is a person and a symbol of One who will rescue us all. The book of Judges is like an anthology series, with each chapter telling the same story. God raises to save the people of Israel time and time again after they fail, after they fall, after they stop listening to the Lord. They cry out to Him for help, salvation, and He sends them a leader, a judge.

The book of Judges speaks of a way out of the mess. It reminds us that we must not do "what is right in our own eyes." Instead, we must follow the King. We hope for a Leader who will bring us the peace and prosperity for which we long. We hold out hope for the Messiah, the King of Kings, the Prince of Peace, who will lead us in ways of truth and happiness.

DEBORAH, A JUDGE IN ISRAEL

Judge is a word we still use today. We think of courtrooms, lawyers, and people in black robes who interpret the law. But that wasn't what a judge was anciently. A judge was more like a warrior, a tribal leader who the Lord would send to rescue them when things got bleak. In Judges 2 we learn:

> Whenever the Lord raised up judges for them, the Lord was with the judge, and he delivered them from the hand of their enemies all the days of the judge; for the Lord would be moved to pity by their groaning because of those who persecuted and oppressed them. But whenever the judge died, they would relapse and behave worse than their ancestors, following other gods, worshiping them and bowing down to them. They would not drop any of their practices or their stubborn ways. So the anger of the Lord was kindled against Israel; and he said, "Because this people have transgressed my covenant that I commanded their ancestors, and have not obeyed my voice, I will no longer drive out before them any of the nations . . . In order to test Israel, whether or not they would take care to walk in the way of the lord as their ancestors did." (NRSV, Judges 2:18–22)

It was a dark time in Israel when the Lord called judges. The country had not yet been unified. Each tribe, from Ephraim to Judah, ruled themselves. They all struggled on their own to flourish. The surrounding people, from the Philistines, the Hittites, Ammonites, and everyone surrounding Israel warred, fought, battled, and caused trouble. The Israelites didn't help themselves. They intermarried, forgot the Lord, and generally got in trouble as fast as possible.

War was common. Canaan was dangerous. It was a tough place to live and raise a family. Far to the north, we meet a woman—a judge called Deborah.

Setting

Far to the north, in the hill country of Ephraim, Deborah sits under a palm tree, giving judgments to the people and resolving disputes. She is also a prophetess. She is gifted of the Lord, discerning His will for the people. She has an additional title: "Woman of Torches." It probably means that she's a charismatic leader with a fiery attitude. Here we have a woman who hears the Spirit of the Lord and leads her people. She is known to make decisions and judgments. Next, she will be called a warrior. Many titles try and capture the woman—judge, prophet, leader, warrior. Later, she will be called Mother of Israel. This is Deborah.

The Bee

The name Deborah is fascinating. However, we don't know precisely the name's etymology. The Hebrew root gives us some clues. *Dbr* as a verb means "to pronounce or formalize."[1] To say a thing and have it done. It is the exact work you see in Genesis when we read, "God said," and then it happens. For example, "And God said, Let there be light: and there was light" (Genesis 1:3). We get the idea of pronouncement, of fiat, of speaking into being.

Similarly, the word *deborah* describes a bee, like a honeybee. A bee and a spoken word are tied to each other conceptually. When a word is spoken, creation and order appear. It is the opposite of wilderness. After God speaks, it becomes a land of milk and honey, a land of plenty, cultivated and giving life. All that life and cultivation of the land takes place by the mighty power of the bee. Packed into that idea of power and life is Deborah. It is a powerful name.

The Story

It's a time in northern Canaan when Israel is surrounded by its enemies. It has yet to pull together and follow the Lord. They are not yet united as the Kingdom of Israel and Judah. It's a confederacy, a group of tribes loosely connected and surrounded by war. In that setting, a time of war and fear, we are introduced to the

---

1. F. Brown, S. Driver, and C. Briggs, *The Brown-Driver-Briggs Hebrew and English Lexicon* (Boston: Hendrickson Publishers, 2004), 1682, 1683, 1697.

prophet Deborah. She is found under a palm and arbitrating disputes for the people. We meet our next character, Barak.

Barak

We don't know much about Barak, except Deborah calls him in the name of the Lord to lead an army. Deborah comes to Barak and tells him that the Lord has told him that he needs to go out and battle against Sisera, the enemy's general.

Barak and the Battle

Here's where there's a bit of a twist. Barak does not go, but not alone. He says that he will go if Deborah goes with him. Barak is truly worried about his chances against Sisera. He knows that Deborah speaks for God, so with her help, he feels confident. Alone he will not go.

Deborah tells him that as a result, the glory will not go to Barak. In a culture where honor is most important, this is a tough blow. Deborah continues and explains that the glory will go to a woman. You probably think it will be Deborah. But hang on, the story gets better.

Barak gathers his armies. Deborah goes with him. God commands them to take 10,000 men to Mount Tabor and battle the Canaanites. The prophetess reminds Barak that he will not get the glory, but rather a woman will (see Judges 4:6).

Enter a new character in our story—the general of the Canaanites, Sisera. The Israelites, under Barak and Deborah, fight ferociously. Sisera, seeing his army defeated, runs and finds himself at the tent of another woman, Jael. Sisera, exhausted from battle, takes some milk from Jael to drink and lays down to rest. He falls asleep. Jael, seeing the general vulnerable and as a friend to the Israelites, devises a plan. She takes a stake from her tent and, while Sisera sleeps, nails it through his temple and kills him.

Deborah's prophecy and pronouncement about Barak not getting glory indeed go to Jael, as she is the one who defeats the enemy general. She is the leader the people need to defeat their enemies. When Israel was fragmented and surrounded by enemies, the Lord raised two leaders, both women.

One of Deborah's greatest titles is in Judges 5, where she is called Mother of Israel. It may be that she was indeed a parent. The term "mother" may also be symbolic, as she gave life and substance to her nation as a military protector. Judges 5 continues with another song, raising the military victory of Deborah. God of Israel, Mother of Israel.

Two Accounts of Deborah

The victory of Deborah is told in two separate accounts. In Judges 4, it's a narrative, and in Judges 5, it's a poem called the Song of Deborah. The Song of Deborah may be one of the oldest parts of the Hebrew Bible.

The Song of Deborah recounts miracles during the battle. The Lord protects the armies of Barak and Deborah. The song tells of the chaos and of the close battle. The enemy begins to overrun the Israelites. The Lord steps in and defends them by sending a flood. The torrent from Kishon sweeps the armies away (see Judges 5:21). The song even recounts how the stars in heaven, the heavenly hosts, fought against Sisera. The Lord sends a flood, which disables the chariots and allows Israel to win. The song concludes with the heroic depiction of Jael, the warrior woman. She taunts the general's mother. There's no sympathy. These were flawed people who caused much death in destruction.

Songs are powerful communication in the Old Testament. There are sacred songs, like Moses and Miriam's Song of the Sea. Later, some women will celebrate David's military success in song (see 1 Samuel 18:6–7). David was a gifted poet and singer whose music soothed King Saul's troubled soul. David, the man after God's heart, was always singing. He even sang in a cave while hiding to save his own life (see Psalm 57). The psalms are songs sung in lament, worship, and praise. The Song of Deborah retells a great victory over a powerful enemy.

Called

In these two leaders, we can see ourselves. How often have we been called to follow the Lord when it was different than the society around us? In our day, when have we been asked to step up, regardless of the odds? Did we follow Him? Deborah and Jael didn't forget their duty when called to do something unique or different. They answered the Lord's call.

Be like Jael. Be like Deborah.

GIDEON

Gideon is harvesting wheat while hiding in a winepress. The Midianites, the enemies of his people, had attacked over and over again. And while he harvests wheat, Gideon fears their attack. He works his grain while he is hiding. It's there that we begin our story of the mighty Man of Valor known as Gideon.

Following the episode of Deborah, it would be wrong to conclude that peace was held in the land of Israel. While Deborah saved the Israelites, peace could not be maintained. Following Deborah and Barak is the story of another judge. The Israelites fall into a cycle of disobedience. They struggle, and the Lord raises another tribal leader, another warrior, yet this is an unlikely hero. The story of Gideon is the story of someone who learns to have faith in God, despite great fear. This story is a story of learning to trust God.

Beginnings

The beginnings of stories tell us a lot about their characters. We peek into the soul of a character when we look at how they are introduced. When we first meet David, he is not a king. He's the youngest son, and he is out shepherding (see 1 Samuel 17:34–36). Shepherding is not the most glamorous job; it is one of the least.

David, this lowly shepherd, steps up to Goliath and defeats him. His faith and humility will be his greatest allies if he can hold onto them. A shepherd warrior? What a great introduction!

And what about Ezekiel? Conquered by Babylon, he sits on the banks of the canal. Disheartened, away from his people and temple, he is sad and dejected. It is also his birthday but not a regular birthday. It is his thirtieth, the year he would have entered service as a priest. The Babylonian captivity ruined his whole life. He had spent the last thirty years training to be a priest of God, and now, far from the temple, he cannot serve. Unexpectedly, he has a vision of God, and Ezekiel's story is about to take a dramatic turn (see Ezekiel 1). Amazing! Another incredible introduction into one of the greatest prophets of the Old Testament.

And what about Huldah the prophetess? Josiah has found some new scriptures in the temple and wants to ensure they are real. So, he sends them to a woman, a prophet, who confirms their authenticity. Here is a time of apostasy, and yet a woman is directing the word of the Lord (see 2 Kings 22:14–20; 2 Chronicles 34:22–28). Shocking, unique, and surprising.

Gideon's Introduction

How does the story of Gideon, Israel's next defender, begin? Judges 6 starts like this:

> The Israelites did evil in the eyes of the Lord, and for seven years he gave them into the hands of the Midianites. Because the power of Midian was so oppressive, the Israelites prepared shelters for themselves in mountain clefts, caves and strongholds. Whenever the Israelites planted their crops, the Midianites, Amalekites and other eastern peoples invaded the country. They camped on the land and ruined the crops all the way to Gaza and did not spare a living thing for Israel, neither sheep nor cattle nor donkeys. They came up with their livestock and their tents like swarms of locusts. It was impossible to count them or their camels; they invaded the land to ravage it. Midian so impoverished the Israelites that they cried out to the Lord for help.

The Israelites are struggling. They have forgotten their covenants and stopped obeying the law. They do not have God's protection. As such, they are overrun by enemies. They have to hide in caves and holes. Their crops are raided, and they are constantly invaded. They are continually fighting off enemies, struggling to raise their families in peace. God is loving and gracious, however. And He hears their cries for help.

The angel of the Lord comes and sits down under the oak in Ophrah that belonged to Joash the Abiezrite, where their son Gideon was threshing wheat in a winepress to keep it from the Midianites. The angel of the Lord appears to Gideon and says, "The Lord is with you, mighty warrior" (NRSV, Judges 6:11–12).

God sends a messenger, an angel, to call a new judge and defender. He finds Gideon hiding while harvesting. The verse says he is in a winepress. This is odd. A winepress is a small, circular pit used to drain the juice out of pressed grapes. Using it to harvest wheat would be a challenge and not very effective. However, the winepress gives Gideon a bit of protection from the Midianites. Just a few feet below ground, he might not be seen.

The angel's greeting seems even more peculiar. The angel of the Lord calls him "mighty warrior" or, in some translations, "mighty man of valor." Gideon doesn't seem very brave. He seems the opposite. God knows something about Gideon that maybe he doesn't even know.

Zooming In

The Lord uses an unexpected technique to teach us, and He is doing it right here. Have you ever wondered where God is during times of significant crisis? Have you ever asked, "During war and famine, where is God?" God teaches us about the world by zooming in on one person or one family. The "picture" starts out by showing us the big view. In Gideon's time, the people are unfaithful. As a result, their enemies have power over them. The people must hide. They cannot farm for food without being overtaken. We see the big picture and what is happening. Then, we zoom in on one person, one family, one story.

That's odd, isn't it? One minute we are hearing about all the terror and horror that is going on. We're learning about the war and the resultant issues. It feels like we are watching the news. Then, in an instant, we are introduced to one person. It is kind of non-sequitur. But it isn't. The big picture and the little picture are related. God shows us that the issues in our world are intimately related and solved by individuals. The Lord answers our question, "Where is God during a crisis?" by showing us what He does one person at a time. He shows us how His Spirit can change one person, and they can change the world.

Here, in answer to cries of the people in Israel, the Lord introduces us to a man hiding in a winepress.

Gideon questions whether the Lord is with His people. In his small-minded view, Gideon doesn't understand the big picture. It is clear with Gideon's following comments to the angel:

> "Pardon me, my lord," Gideon replied, "but if the Lord is with us, why has all this happened to us? Where are all his wonders that our ancestors told us about when they said, 'Did not the Lord bring us up out of Egypt?' But now the Lord has abandoned us and given us into the hand of Midian."
>
> The Lord turned to him and said, "Go in the strength you have and save Israel out of Midian's hand. Am I not sending you?"
>
> "Pardon me, my lord," Gideon replied, "but how can I save Israel? My clan is the weakest in Manasseh, and I am the least in my family."
>
> The Lord answered, "I will be with you, and you will strike down all the Midianites, leaving none alive." (NRSV, Judges 6:13–16)

Gideon thought that God had abandoned them. Gideon could only see the terrible events in his life and concluded that the Lord was not aware of him. Or perhaps he felt like God was like a "cosmic butler" at the people's beck and call to bring them only blessings. Gideon mistakenly thought that God alone was responsible for everything happening in his life. Since war covered the land, Gideon had doubts. Gideon did not yet understand the Lord's power, His blessing, and the responsibility each person has to do good.

Gideon reveals something common in many of us—the ability to only see God during the good times. Gideon had grown up with stories about the Passover, the crossing of the sea, and the wonders in the times of Moses. For Gideon, those examples were in the distant past. God may have performed wonders or miracles for them, but where were the good times? Where were the blessings, miracles, abundance, and signs in his day? You see, Gideon thought God was only "with" him when he could see the good things, the marvels, and the wonders. God is going to teach Gideon that He is with him all of the time.

With You

In just a few short verses the term "with you/us" is used. The angel says, "The Lord is *with you,* mighty warrior" (NRSV, Judges 6:11–12; emphasis added).

Then, Gideon questions it with, "Pardon me, my lord . . . but if the Lord is *with us*, why has all this happened to us? (NRSV, Judges 6:13).

Only a verse or so later the Lord replies, "I will be *with you*" (NRSV, Judges 6:16; emphasis added).

This verbal fencing is Gideon arguing, fighting with the Lord. He does not see any "signs." He only sees the mayhem and tyranny of his enemies. He mistakenly thinks that the Lord, as covenant partner, is *only* with him when things are going well. Unless there are miracles and magic, great blessings, and wonders, Gideon does not see the Lord. What Gideon fails to realize is that a covenant relationship means that God is "abounding in steadfast love and faithfulness, keeping steadfast love for the thousandth generation" (NRSV, Exodus 34:6). We will see the Lord show Gideon how He is "with him."

Gideon also tells us something interesting about himself. He is the "least." Gideon comes from the smallest tribe, a minor family within that tribe, and he's the "least in [his] family." Alone, he does not stand a chance. This will also be important in seeing God's hand in Gideon's and the Israelites' lives.

Callings and Tests

Gideon has doubts. Right from the start, he questions and asks for multiple signs. First, he prepares a meal and takes it back to the angel. The angel has him set it on a rock. Then, touching the food with his staff, a miracle happens. Flame flares from the rock and consumes the food. Gideon is in awe and says, "Alas, Sovereign Lord! I have seen the angel of the Lord face to face" (NRSV, Judges 6:22). Gideon has seen a great sign and seems to recognize it immediately. He begins to understand and receives his first calling. He is to go into town and destroy the idol and altar to Ba'al. But it isn't just any altar—it is his father's.

Gideon gathers some of his friends and sets out to perform the task. But he doesn't do it like he was told. He goes at night. He is afraid the villagers will kill him. When the town realizes their altar is torn down, they investigate and find out it was Gideon. They march out to kill him. Luckily, Gideon's father stands up for him, and the crisis is averted.

The story only gets stranger from here.

Bigger Assignments

Gideon has met an angel. He's had a miraculous sign. He has also had an assignment that, despite some dicey moments, works out. Now, Gideon is getting a more significant project. There is a large army of Israel's enemies on their way to destroy them. Our hero is to gather an army and meet them. Yet, Gideon still doubts. He asks the angel to perform three more signs to prove that Gideon will prevail. The story takes an unexpected turn. Gideon requests three more signs. Gideon still doubts after seeing an angel, a miracle with food consumed by fire, and being protected from the idolatrous villagers.

A Sign or Two, or Four

We have always heard that asking for a sign is wicked. We have also learned that faith precedes the miracle. It would seem those are all true. Gideon is still full of fear. Then he asks for another kind of miracle.

Remember, Gideon has only known war and terror. He has not seen God's hand, His grace, in his life.

> Gideon said to God, "If you will save Israel by my hand as you have promised—look, I will place a wool fleece on the threshing floor. If there is dew only on the fleece and all the ground is dry, then I will know that you will save Israel by my hand, as you said." And that is what happened. Gideon rose early the next day; he squeezed the fleece and wrung out the dew—a bowlful of water. (NRSV, Judges 6:36–38)

Gideon has asked for another sign, an additional miracle to confirm that God will defend him in battle. Is he *really* supposed to defend Israel? he wonders. This miracle is a gift to inspire confidence. Gideon is not convinced.

> Then Gideon said to God, "Do not be angry with me. Let me make just one more request. Allow me one more test with the fleece, but this time make the fleece dry and let the ground be covered with dew." That night God did so. Only the fleece was dry; all the ground was covered with dew. (NRSV, Judges 6:39–40)

Gideon sets the fleece out, and, of course, God does the miracle, this time in reverse from the first. Finally, Gideon is convinced and sets out to raise an army to defend Israel.

This may seem a little strange to us. We probably think that we would obey the Lord on any sign that He gave us, that after seeing something miraculous, we would jump up and act. We hope we will be faithful and trust God. But isn't this a little bit like us?

Don't we often see miraculous things? Haven't we heard of miraculous and wondrous things that the Lord has done in the past and our day, our own families, and in our own lives? And yet we continue to ask. I love that the Lord still answers and reassures Gideon.

You know the story's a little bit strange. We've heard that it is. It shows a lack of faith that we have to ask for a sign. Gideon keeps asking for additional signs, too. We might be tempted to think Gideon is weak. He might be. But I believe the Lord's telling us something else in this story. What's clear about this story is that Gideon has real fear. Gideon is apprehensive about these enormous tasks that he's been asked to do. He wants a little comfort and more reassurance.

There's an application here for us. When we are asked to do something hard, something that scares us, we wonder, is this from God? It's okay to ask. It's okay to ask again and again. It is all right to get reassurance on the things the Lord's asking us to do. He doesn't seem upset about that. Gideon keeps asking for these confirmations, and he keeps getting them. I wonder if the Lord didn't include this story because we are all a little bit like Gideon. We might be new to hearing Him. We might be asked to do something scary. We might not be sure the Spirit is guiding us. We have things we're not sure we're up for. We have assignments, callings, a life that we don't know we can do. We just want to be completely sure that this is what the Lord desires, that the Lord is on our side. There are times we need to confirm that we are acting the way the Lord has instructed. The Lord does not chastise Gideon, and He doesn't withhold the miracles. The Lord blesses Gideon with the confirmation he needs. We are blessed with priesthood leaders to help guide and direct us. And if Gideon's story is any indication, I think the Lord will give us the signs we need, too.

Gideon is learning what a covenant relationship with God is like. He has assumed it is about good things—blessing and miracles. He fails to see that God was with Israel, even when they sinned and left the covenant path. The challenges, the war, are also a sign of the covenant. God does not want us to suffer; that is not the point. However, as a result of the Israelites failing to keep the terms of the agreement, they do not have God's protection. This, too, shows God is aware of them. And God is ready to welcome them back.

The Last Signs

As Gideon prepares to defend Israel, he calls for the Israelites to help. Thirty-three thousand men gather to put down the threat of the Midianites. Then, Gideon receives a new command from the Lord.

> You have too many men. I cannot deliver Midian into their hands, or Israel would boast against me, "My own strength has saved me." Now announce to the army, "Anyone who trembles with fear may turn back and leave Mount Gilead." So twenty-two thousand men left, while ten thousand remained. (NRSV, Judges 7:2–3)

Gideon has done what he was asked. He has raised an army, but God tells him it is too many. Any men who are afraid can leave. Remarkably, they do. Twenty-two thousand men leave. Then, God says,

> "There are still too many men. Take them down to the water, and I will thin them out for you there. If I say, 'This one shall go with you,' he shall go; but if I say, 'This one shall not go with you,' he shall not go."
>
> So Gideon took the men down to the water. There the Lord told him, "Separate those who lap the water with their tongues as a dog laps from those who kneel down to drink." Three hundred of them drank from cupped hands, lapping like dogs. All the rest got down on their knees to drink.
>
> The Lord said to Gideon, "With the three hundred men that lapped I will save you and give the Midianites into your hands. Let all the others go home." (NRSV, Judges 7:4–7)

God asks Gideon to dismiss even more men. Now only three hundred remain to stand against the entire army of the Midianites. What is God doing?

Night Battle

During the night, God instructs Gideon to approach the camp of the Midianites. He gives each of his men a trumpet, a *shofar,* the horn of a ram, and a torch. Night battles are not expected. Nobody can see. You are just as likely to injure or attack your army at night. These are not the days of special equipment like infrared and night vision goggles. We should be thinking, "What is going on here?"

Each of the men takes a clay jar and puts a torch hidden inside so the light is covered. Then Gideon divides the three hundred men into three groups. At his command, they blow their shofars, scream their battle cry, and shine the light of their torches. The three groups, torches and horns blazing, go screaming into the army of the Midianites. You can only imagine the chaos. It is night. The Midianites do not expect a night attack. They hear trumpets, they hear men screaming, and they think that it's not three hundred me, but thousands, and that each man is representing the torch of many men.

The men cry out their battle cry, "For the Lord! For Gideon." We now know that God is fighting for Israel. Outnumbered, through the power of the Lord they defend their homes. Gideon has become a mighty man of valor. When the angel greets him in the beginning, he is hiding. He is fearful. The Lord knows something about Gideon that Gideon does not know. The Lord knows that inside him is a brave man. Indeed, with God, we can all become mighty. Indeed, Gideon is a mighty man of valor. Gideon and the Lord gain a triumphant victory over the army.

After such a great battle, the people cry for Gideon to become their king. Humble as always, he says, "No, the Lord is your king."

God Knew Something about Gideon

God knows something about Gideon that maybe Gideon doesn't know about himself. And it isn't just one story or one event that gives Gideon the faith to act. The Lord repeatedly coaxes, cajoles, pushes, and encourages Gideon to become the savior of his nation.

Sometimes we forget that God works with fearful people. People who need a sign, or three, before they can act. In reducing the number of men in battle, by creating a unique battle plan, God is sending a sign that He is with them.

Have you ever doubted a sign you've been given? Even after all that we've seen—all the miracles, blessings, and wonders—do we still hesitate? I think we do. And, if Gideon is an example, I believe the Lord is okay with that. He knows that our lives are scary at times. We face insurmountable forces arrayed against us, and we might need a push to engage. Gideon checks four times that it is *really* a sign. There are times when we can double-check our answers, ask for confirmation, and let the Lord know we are scared.

I wonder if, like Gideon, sometimes we don't precisely follow like we are asked. When Gideon is commanded to go and throw down the altar of Ba'al, he knows he is risking his life. Even though he believes in the Lord, he knows it might not end well. So, he gathers up some of his friends and goes at night when it is safer.

It's a good message to us. God has given us some friends that we can call on when we're faced with a big task. They may be your family members, those in your ward or branch, or students in your seminary or institute class. You've got friends in the Lord. And what about going at night? Well, perhaps it doesn't show perfect faith, but Gideon still does it.

There are certainly times when we don't follow through on a commandment precisely as we thought we should. It could be that we hesitated to act, went on a mission a few years late, accepted that calling we'd been worried about, or asked someone for forgiveness that we wronged long ago. Gideon's story shows us that God accepts what we can do, even if all we can do is show up. And it's okay to bring some friends along the way.

How does Gideon's story end? With just a few, the Lord defeats the enemies of Gideon, and the Israelites are saved. I like this message. Even if I don't always see how it will work out, even when it seems like we are outnumbered and the plan is a little sketchy (torches and horns at night), the Lord has a significant outcome.

What are the night-time attacks in your life? When have you been asked to put a torch in a pot and attack with a horn? When has the Lord asked you to do something that seems too little, too strange, or bound to fail? I think Gideon's story is something we may all face.

I pray that we can all remember the lessons of Gideon whenever these situations arise in our lives:

- A night-time assault: Remember Gideon.
- A small amount of support: Remember Gideon.
- Outnumbered and overwhelmed: Remember Gideon.
- A unique battle plan: Remember Gideon.

When you feel overwhelmed and outnumbered, when you are anxious and fearful when the Lord's request seems odd or unique, remember Gideon. In our good times and in our bad, when we can see God's signs in our lives and when we cannot, we can remember His covenant promises. And then you too can shout the fierce battle cry: "For the Lord! For Gideon!"

RUTH

Tasks fill our days. Each moment of our lives are seemingly packed with regular, pedantic, boring stuff. To exist in the twenty-first century, we have a lot of responsibility and a lot to do. We have to work or go to school. We wake up, brush our teeth, drive, and eat, only to repeat it day after day. Some days are filled with chores like mowing the lawn, taking out the garbage, and cleaning. Other days all we do is go to work or school, eat, and rush to an event or social gathering, only to repeat it the next day. Our days are busy and sometimes monotonous.

The stories of the scriptures are filled with miraculous, unique, action-packed events. Situations like Moses parting the sea, Nephi building a boat, Joseph having a vision, or the Savior healing a blind man are on each page. The scriptures can show us the stories of incredible events, of prophets and kings, warriors, and rebels. We see God acting in dramatic ways in their lives, like speaking from a burning bush or curing a plague. In short, those scripture stories don't seem much like our lives, do they?

We watch those larger-than-life examples of God working to save and redeem His family. We look at our own lives filled with routine tasks and wonder, "Where is God in my life? Is He in my story? How is He working to save and redeem me?" Often in our lives, God's presence is more subtle. In the busy work of living, it can be hard to see God's hand. Have you ever wondered if you matter, if the daily grind on endless repeat is different from God's big story?

Keep reading. The book of Ruth is for you.

THE STORY, CHAPTER 1

A long time ago, during the days when the Judges led Israel, there was a terrible famine. Elimelech and his wife, Naomi, lived in Bethlehem. Famine struck the land, and Elimelech and Naomi took their two sons and moved to Moab in search of food. Disaster struck, and Elimelech died, leaving Naomi and their two sons.[1] For ten more years, Naomi and her sons lived in Moab. They married Moabite women and started to settle down. When all seemed to be going well, the two sons of Naomi died. Disaster! Naomi was left without her husband and sons, in a land that wasn't her own.

BACKDROP

It is the time of the Judges. It is a dark time, a time of anarchy and war, famine, and destruction. We have already read a little about a couple of judges, Deborah and Gideon, but it is worth reviewing. After the Exodus, the deliverance from bondage in Egypt, the people fall away again. They forget the Lord. The Lord feels compassion for the people, so He raises a judge (think more like tribal leader or hero, not a lawyer or someone in a courtroom).

> Whenever the Lord raised up judges for them, the Lord was with the judge, and he delivered them from the hand of their enemies all the days of the judge; for the Lord would be moved to pity by their groaning because of those who persecuted and oppressed them. But whenever the judge died, they would relapse and behave worse than their ancestors, following other gods, worshiping them and bowing down to them. They would not drop any of their practices or their stubborn ways . . . In order to test Israel, whether or not they would

---

1. Mahlon and Kilion. Their names make more sense in Hebrew and show how they won't last long. They were probably not the real names of the sons but rather narrative tools. Here is the meaning of the names in the story: Elimelech: God is my king; Mahlon: Sickness; Kilion: Death; Naomi: Pleasantness; Boaz: Strength; Ruth: Friend.

take care to walk in the way of the Lord as their ancestors did. (NRSV, Judges 2:18–19, 22)

Sounds familiar, doesn't it? The cycle of pride was present even then. The people will be blessed and prosper. Then, just when they are being blessed, they will let pride creep in. Disobedience and sin will return. They will ignore the Lord's commandments, and so they will become oppressed and overwhelmed. They will be humbled and remember Him. The Lord will bless them, "for the Lord would be moved to pity by their groaning because of those who persecuted and oppressed them" (2:18). Even though the people have seen great miracles, they forget the Lord, and war and famine cover the land.

Setting

Naomi and her family are from Bethlehem, which is west of the Dead Sea in the foothills of the hill country. It is where Jesus will be born about one thousand years later. The city of Jerusalem, which isn't quite Jerusalem yet, is to the northeast.

Across the River Jordan, to the north and the east, is the land of Moab. The Moabites and the Israelites, who are enemies, have fought and warred for a couple hundred years.

Naomi and Elimelech experience a terrible famine. So, to escape and survive, they move their family, including their two sons, to Moab in search of food. But disaster strikes the little family. First, the father and then the two sons die. Only Naomi and her two Moabite daughters-in-law are left. They have no family support. In those days, it was challenging for women to survive alone without a tribe or extended family.

Now, back to the story.

NAOMI RETURNS TO BETHLEHEM

Naomi decides to return home—she has no other choice. She packs up her two daughters-in-law, Orpah and Ruth, and begins the trek back to Bethlehem in the land of Judah. She has heard that God has blessed the land there and that they have food again. She has nothing and is starving.

After a short time on the road, Naomi turns to her two daughters-in-law and says, "Go back. Go home and live with your mothers. And May God treat you as graciously as you have treated your deceased husbands and me. May God give each of you a new home and a new husband." She kisses them and they weep. They say, "No, we're going to go on with you, to your people." But Naomi is firm and says, "Go back, my dear daughters. Why would you come with me? Go back, dear daughters—on your way, please! No, my daughter. It would be far better for me than for you because the hand of the Lord has turned against me." They all weep. Orpah kisses her mother-in-law and leaves to return home to Moab.

Naomi is sure that all of this has happened to her because God has forgotten her. But what about Ruth? Will she stay and help Naomi or return to her people? She turns to Naomi and says,

"Do not press me to leave you or to turn back from following you!
Where you go, I will go;
where you lodge, I will lodge;
your people shall be my people,
and your God, my God.
17 Where you die, I will die—
there will I be buried.
May the Lord do thus and so to me,
and more as well,
if even death parts me from you!" (NRSV, Ruth 1:16–17)

When Naomi sees that Ruth has her heart set on going with her, she gives in, and so the two travel on together to Bethlehem. When they arrive in Bethlehem, the whole town is abuzz, saying, "Is this really Naomi after all this time?"

Naomi is struggling under the burden of losing her family. She tells the townspeople, "Don't call me Naomi. Call me *Mara* or Bitter. The Almighty has dealt me a bitter blow. I left here full of life, and God has brought me back with nothing but the clothes on my back. Why would you call me pleasant? God certainly doesn't. The Almighty has ruined me."

What Is Going On?

Ruth is a Moabite. We may be suspicious of her. Her people are our enemies. She is different from her Israelite neighbors. Naomi asks her to return to her parents because they are destitute. She can no longer support her. The family is broken. We can hardly slight Orpah when she decided to leave. A Moabite in the land of Judah would have been very unwelcome.[2]

What of Ruth? Who is this woman? In a few short phrases, we learn everything we need to know about Ruth.

> "Where you go, I will go;
> where you lodge, I will lodge;
> your people shall be my people,
> and your God my God." (NRSV, Ruth 1:16)

Ruth chooses to stay and live and die with her mother-in-law. She also decides to follow the Lord. She shows her dedication to duty and love to help the older woman, even with no prospects. Ruth also knows that moving to Bethlehem means she is choosing to follow the Lord. This is a declaration of faith.

Despite Ruth's beautiful assertion of faith and dedication, all seems lost.

This story is like all our stories. At times when we are without support. Maybe we have lost our jobs, moved to a new country, or have no friends. Perhaps there are times when we have no one to

---

2. This is the legend of Oprah Winfrey, the media Mogul. Her name was biblical, referring to this very story. However, since no one was sure how to spell or pronounce it, they started calling her Oprah. She could have been Orpah Winfrey this whole time (Interview with Oprah Winfrey, BBC Radio 4, https://www.bbc.co.uk/programmes/b09lvy4s. Originally broadcast Sat., Jan. 13, 2018; accessed 10/5/2021).

turn to—when we are lost, alone, and unsure where to go next. Men or women, we all have times in our lives when we are like Naomi. When bitterness threatens to overcome us, when we feel alone and helpless, we are Naomi.

When is a time in your life when you were lost? Maybe it was financially. Perhaps it was spiritually or emotionally. At times we all feel truly alone and hopeless.

It can be hard to see God's hand in our lives. When we are burdened by death and disaster, when we are suffering and can see no hope, it is then that we ask, "Where is God?" Naomi is sure that the Lord has forgotten her. How else do we explain what has happened to her? As she asks the question, we should ask ourselves the same. Where is God, not only during the pedantic but during the tedious tasks of our lives? Where is He when things go wrong? Naomi doesn't know yet in her story. Let's keep reading to find out the answer.

Have we ever been like Ruth? Have we been asked to stay loyal, to choose the God of Israel when everything was telling us to choose something, anything, else? When life gets tough, will we be Ruth and commit to the Lord when we are at a crossroads?

THE STORY, CHAPTER 2

Enter a New Character, Boaz

It just so happens that Naomi has a distant relative by marriage, Boaz. He is prominent and prosperous and connected to her husband's family.

Ruth needs a plan to herself and Naomi, so she tells Naomi, "I'm going to go to work. I'm going to go out and harvest barley from the sheaves that are leftover from some harvester who won't give me a hard time and will treat me kindly." Ruth sets out and starts gleaning in the field, following in the wake of the harvesters. Eventually, she ends up in the part of the field owned by Boaz.

A little later, Boaz comes out from Bethlehem, greeting his harvesters. "God be with you!"

They reply, "And God bless you."

Boaz notices a young woman in the field. He asks his foreman, "Who is that young women woman? Where did she come from?"

And the foreman says, "Well, that's the Moabite girl, the one who came with Naomi. She asked permission to glean among the sheaves following after harvesters. She's been at it steady ever since from early morning until now."

Boaz speaks to Ruth. "Listen, my daughter, from now on, you don't need to go to the other fields to glean. Stay right here in this one. Then stay close to my young women. Watch where they are harvesting. Follow them. You don't need to worry about a thing. I've given orders to my servants not to harass you. If you get thirsty, feel free to go drink from the water buckets that the servants have filled."

Ruth falls her knees and bows, her face to the ground. "How does this happen that you should pick me out and treat me so kindly? Me, a foreigner?"

And Boaz answers, "I've heard all about you! I've heard about the way you treated your mother-in-law after the death of her husband! How you left your father and your mother and the land of your birth and have come to live among total strangers." He looks at her kindly. "God reward you well for what you've done and with a full reward—the Lord to whom you've come seeking protection under His wings."

And she says, "Oh, sir, such grace, such kindness. I don't deserve it! You've touched my heart, treated me like one of your own. And I don't even belong here!"

After the lunch break, Boaz says to her, "Come over here. Eat some bread. Dip it in the vinegar." Ruth joins the harvesters. Boaz passes the food to her. Ruth eats until she is full and is even given some leftovers. When she gets up to go back to work, Boaz orders his servants, "Let her glean were there is still plenty of grain on the ground. Make it easy for her. Better yet, pull some of the good stuff out and leave it for her to pick up. Don't make it hard for her."

Ruth gleans in the field until the evening, when she threshes out what she has gathered. She ends up with nearly a whole sack of barley. She goes back into town and shows her mother-in-law the results of her day's work. She gives Naomi the leftovers from her lunch.

Naomi asks her, "Where did you work gleaning today? Whose field? God bless, whoever it was who took such good care of you."

Ruth tells her mother-in-law, "The man with whom I worked today? His name is Boaz."

Naomi says to her daughter in law, "Why, God bless that man! God did not walk out on us after all. He still loves us in bad times as well as good!" She continues, "That man, Ruth, is one of our Kindred Redeemers, a close relative of ours."

Ruth the Moabite says, "Well, listen to this. He also told me, 'Stick with my workers until my harvesting is finished.'"

Naomi says to Ruth, "That's wonderful, dear daughter. Do that. You'll be safe in the company of those young women. No danger now of being attacked in some stranger's field."

So, Ruth does it. She sticks close to Boaz's workers, gleaning in the fields until the barley and harvest are complete. Ruth continues living with and supporting her mother-in-law.

Boaz, the Kinsman Redeemer

Now we meet Boaz. He is a prosperous landowner with fields and many workers. However, he is more than that. He is also a righteous and moral man who is able "to bring Yahweh's blessing to his people and Ruth" (Ruth 2:4, 12). When Boaz calls out a blessing from Jehovah, it indicates that he is faithful to the Lord. He, as a righteous man, can bring blessings. When the servants respond, we know that Boaz is worthy of love and respect. He is a rich man, but more important, he is a kind and faithful follower of the Lord.

We see Boaz's kindness in his exchange with Ruth. When she protests that he knows who she is, we learn that he knows all about her. He recounts how he is aware that Ruth is a Moabite and caring for her widowed mother-in-law. Boaz is a mighty and meek man, a man with great power that he uses for blessing the people around him.

The people call him Kinsman Redeemer, a term we do not use today but that was part of the law. The Kinsman Redeemer, sometimes just called Redeemer, had several responsibilities. He could buy back the land or home sold to cover debt (see Leviticus 25:33, 27:15; Deuteronomy 10:18). After a family member had sold himself into slavery (or been sold), the Kindred Redeemer was responsible for paying the price to release, or redeem, him. In addition, the male relative could "redeem" a widow who was left behind with no child by marriage. Through the Kinsman Redeemer the Israelites helped the widow, the orphan, and the poor. This family member could give relief to those who were in bondage, but it had a cost. The Redeemer had to take on the debt, pay the price, and continue to care for those they had redeemed.

Israelite Welfare

Every society has people who need support. The Israelites were to give special care to the widow, orphan, immigrant, and poor (see Exodus 22:22, 23:6,11; Leviticus 25:25, 35, 39, 47–48; Deuteronomy 10:18, 24:14, 17; and many more). The Lord made way for those who were marginalized and disadvantaged to have food. Israelites were instructed to leave the corners of their fields unharvested. In addition, they were to do a single pass on gathering the grain, olives, or grapes. That way, anyone could harvest the fields' corners or go back and pick up any leavings (see Exodus 23:11; Leviticus 19:10). In Deuteronomy we read:

> When you are harvesting in your field, and you overlook a sheaf, do not go back to get it. Leave it for the alien, the fatherless, and the widow so that the Lord your God may bless you in all the work of

your hands. When you beat the olives from your trees, do not go over the branches a second time. Leave what remains for the alien, the fatherless, and the widow. When you harvest the grapes in your vineyard, do not go over the vines again. Leave what remains for the alien, the fatherless and the widow. (NRSV, 24:19–21).

God gives the people a way to work for themselves and be supported. And they could be sustained, so there would never be anyone starving in the land of Israel.

What does this say about Boaz? He not only follows the law, but he makes it easier for Ruth. Boaz does more than the law requires. He shows real generosity. Boaz knows Ruth is supporting Naomi, is vulnerable in society as a young woman, and is a foreigner. It says something about Boaz that he not only follows this practice, but he does so every day and is generous, too.

Threshing Floor, Barley, and Chaff

So, what's up with all the agricultural references? I did not grow up on a farm, and I'm guessing you didn't either (at least, not an ancient Israelite farm). The author didn't explain what these things are because they knew that everyone would know the references. We don't explain context when we know everyone understands it. For example, I don't explain what goes into a Thanksgiving dinner. I just say, "We were so full after Thanksgiving, we slept for an hour on the floor." Since you have probably overeaten at American Thanksgiving dinner, or at least know the reference, I don't have to explain how much we eat on that holiday. Understanding the nuances and details of a holiday about family, football, and food is context. In ancient Israel, or at least rural farming, we might need a little context.

The book of Ruth is full of ancient farming references. In addition to reaping, which is picking up the grain stocks, there is talk of a threshing floor. First, the grain is taken to a threshing floor. Usually, a circular surface of stone or cobbles is formed in a circle. Sometimes there is a low wall around it, or even a covering or barn.

The harvested stalks of grain are placed on the hard surface, and a threshing-board is stomped, dragged, or otherwise pushed over the top of the grain. The grain is then broken off from the stalk. Once that's done, the worker tosses the grain into the air with a winnowing fork. From there, the grain can be gathered. (Trivia note: to keep the grain from falling out of the barn or the threshing floor, a board was placed across the doorway, called a threshold).

Boaz's harvest is finished. After all the hard work, the grain is gathered, the famine is over, and Ruth and Naomi have food. But where is this story going? And where is God in this story?

So, What's the Point?

In Israel, as well as today, tragedy can strike. Here we have Naomi and Ruth, two widows. Men were the protectors and landowners of the family, and without them, the women were especially vulnerable. Piling on to the death of three family members, Naomi is in Moab, a land of her enemies.

Boaz is a good man. He obeys the commandments every day. He goes out of his way to help the widows, supporting them, protecting them, and watching out for them. He loves God and his neighbor. He is acting like a true Israelite, a man of the covenant.

Now's a good time to point out the question hanging over us: "Where is God?" There are a lot of details, even tragedy, in their lives. What is God doing about it? While we can't see Him influencing the events directly, we start to see how the pieces of Naomi, Ruth, and Boaz's lives are being moved.

THE STORY, CHAPTER 3

One day Ruth's mother-in-law, Naomi, says, "Ruth, my dear daughter, isn't it about time I arranged for a good home for you so that you can be secure and happy? And isn't Boaz the one with whom you've been working? Maybe it's time to make a move. Tonight is the night of Boaz's barley harvest at the threshing floor.

So, take a bath, and put on some perfume. You don't have to show you are in mourning anymore but that you're now available. Get dressed up when you go to the threshing floor tonight. I have a plan."

Naomi tells Ruth her plan. "Don't let Boaz know you're there until the party is underway. After Boaz is done eating and drinking and settles into sleep, lie down at his feet and let him know you're available for marriage."

Ruth agrees to the plan. She dresses up, goes to the threshing floor, and does precisely as Naomi suggested. Boaz has had a good time. The harvest is in, and after all the hard work and feasting on a big meal, he settles into sleep at the end of a barley stack. Wrapped in his cloak, he notices when his feet got cold and are sticking out. And there, at his feet, is Ruth. Startled, he asks, "Who are you?"

"I am Ruth, your servant. Take me under your protective wing. You're my Kindred Redeemer. We could marry!"

Boaz says, "God bless you, my dear! What a splendid expression of love when you could have had your pick of any of the younger (and more handsome) men. Don't you worry about a thing; I will do what you ask. Everyone knows you are a courageous woman!" Boaz is so honest. He knows another relative is closer to Naomi, so he could buy back the land and save the family. Boaz mentions this and says he will let this unknown relative step up. But if he doesn't, Boaz will marry her. So, he takes his cloak and spreads it over the two of them like wings.

She prepares to leave early in the morning, and Boaz sends her off with food for Naomi. Ruth goes home and reports back to Naomi, who says, "Sit still, my daughter, everything will be wrapped up by the end of the day."

What Is It All About?

Here we see the character of Boaz. He is a rich man. He has a large harvest, God's blessing after the famine, and shares it with his servants. After a feast, he stays there, undoubtedly, to guard the grain. Full and exhausted, he lays down to sleep.

Our second interaction between Boaz and Ruth takes place. Boaz is not as young and good-looking as some of the other men. While some see him as a prosperous landowner, he sees himself as someone who missed out. Boaz does the right thing because it is the right thing to do. He consistently does the right thing, day in and day out. Every day, he is kind, generous, and honors God. But he isn't the alpha male, isn't the most popular, has never been married, and sees himself as just average. So, he is surprised to have Ruth pay attention to him, a beautiful and hard-working, faithful, and loyal woman. How could he deserve someone like Ruth?

And Ruth? The story sounds like a romantic comedy. Will they get together? Or what about this other relative? Will he jump in and get involved?

Let's recap: Ruth would have been clothed and mourning. Naomi can see what is going on, that Boaz will fall for Ruth. Ruth needs to indicate that she is available. She takes off her mourning clothes, dresses up, wears make-up again, does up her hair, and heads to the threshing floor. After all the hard work of the harvest, the workers will eat a huge meal, drink, and celebrate the end of the season.

THE STORY, CHAPTER 4

Boaz immediately leaves and heads to the gates of the city. He waits there for the "close relative" to pass by.

"Step aside, old friend," says Boaz. "Take a seat." The man sits down. Then Boaz gathers ten of the city elders. "Sit down here with us; we've got some business to take care of." And they sit down. Boaz says to the relative, "The piece of property that belongs to our relative Elimelech is being sold by his widow, Naomi, who has just returned from the country of Moab. I thought you ought to know about it. Buy it back if you want it—you can make it official in the presence of those sitting here and before the town elders. You have first redeemer rights. If you don't want it, tell me so I'll know where you stand. You're first in line to do this, and I'm next after you."

He says, "I'll buy it."

Then Boaz adds, "You realize, don't you, that when you buy the field from Naomi, you also get Ruth the Moabite, the widow of our dead relative, along with the redeemer responsibility to have children with her to carry on the family inheritance."

Then the relative says, "Oh, I can't do that. I'd jeopardize my own family's inheritance. You go ahead and buy it. You can have my rights. I can't do it."

Boaz then addresses the elders and all the people in the town square that day: "You are witnesses today that I have bought from Naomi everything that belonged to Elimelech and Kilion and Mahlon, including responsibility for Ruth, the foreigner. I'll take her as my wife and keep the deceased's name alive along with his inheritance. The memory and reputation of the deceased are not going to disappear out of this family of his hometown. To all this, you are witnesses this very day."

All the townspeople, the witnesses at the gate, say, "We are witnesses. The Lord make the woman that is come into thine house like Rachel and like Leah, which two did build the house of Israel; and do thou worthily and be famous in Bethlehem. Then, Boaz took Ruth as his wife. She conceived, and she had a son."

The town women said to Naomi, "Blessed be God! He didn't leave you without a family to carry on your life. May this baby be famous in Israel! And he shall be a restorer of your life and care for you in your old age. And this daughter-in-law who has brought him into the world loves you so much she is worth more to you than seven sons!"

Naomi takes the child into her arms and cares for him. The neighborhood starts calling him "Naomi's baby boy." But his real name is Obed. He becomes the father of Jesse, who becomes the father of David.

This is the family tree of Perez:
> Perez had Hezron,
> Hezron had Ram,
> Ram had Amminadab,
> Amminadab had Nahshon,
> Nahshon had Salmon,
> Salmon had Boaz,
> Boaz had Obed,
> Obed had Jesse,
> and Jesse had David.

WRAPPING IT UP

The book of Ruth shows how God doesn't only win battles or hold the sun in the sky. In this story, there are no visions or angels. There is no prophet on a hillside, pillars of fire, or voices from heaven. The book of Ruth is a story about lives like ours. Lives of challenge as well as joy. Lives of death and marriage, work, and effort. In this little powerhouse of scripture, we learn that God is present in our lives. More important, we know that our day-to-day decisions to love God and our neighbor can impact the entire world.

When Naomi thinks God has forgotten her, we learn that He is working to bless us. The whole town witnesses, "Blessed be God! He didn't leave you without a family to carry on your life. May this baby be famous in Israel! And he shall be a restorer of your life and care for you." When everything in Naomi's life becomes a struggle, God is working in the background to bless her and all of us.

When Ruth dedicates her life to supporting her mother-in-law and following the Lord, God uses that to bless Naomi. Through those "small and simple things are great things brought to pass" (Alma 37:6). Ruth's faithfulness and hard work turn to bless and support. Ruth chooses to do the right thing, even when she is stereotyped and dismissed as "other."

When Boaz follows the commandments every day and feeds the poor and the immigrant, he becomes a tool in God's hand.

When for the "millionth time" Boaz does the right thing, it makes a difference. As Boaz follows his sacred commitments and keeps his covenants, God is there, behind the scenes, using that faithfulness to change lives.

God isn't mentioned directly in the story. This story is about God working in small and simple ways with regular people, pulling all their actions together to achieve greatness. Ruth's faithfulness and dedication save more than just her mother-in-law. Boaz's faithfulness to God and kindness to the vulnerable make a difference.

When we do the small things, when we are faithful and dedicated, keep the commandments, and follow the covenant path, even when it seems like it makes no difference, God uses us to bless and save the world. Where is God in the story? He is there all along, exactly like He is in our lives, aware of every action, every choice to be faithful. The Lord blesses our lives when we are faithful and serve Him and our neighbor.

Ending with a Bang

The story of Ruth is a fascinating ancient story. Why is it in the scriptures? We have some insights into agriculture, ancient Israelite politics, and welfare systems. But how is the book of Ruth a story about the Savior? How does it fit in? And the last section—that boring genealogy. What is that all about? I bet you skipped it. I don't blame you. A list of old dead relatives is hard to follow.

But here's the thing: That list of genealogy is the *most important* part! Genealogies are like seams in a quilt, where everything comes together. This family has a couple of important names, starting with that last one, David. The book of Judges ended in horror because "in those days there was no king in Israel: every man did that which was right in his own eyes" (Judges 25:21). There was a promise of a king who would bring the people out of misery and war and destruction. It all starts with David.

God takes this story of tragedy—a widow and a foreigner, alone and without support—and blesses their faithfulness. Through Ruth and Boaz, a son is born. Obed (a word that means servant) has a grandson, David, who will be the king of Israel. He is the one who will bring all the tribes together. David will receive a covenant that the Messiah will come through his family (see 2 Samuel 7:5–16). David is the actual king who is a symbol of a future perfect king. Through the line of Ruth and Boaz, a true king, the Messiah, will be born. The Servant will come into the world to save them. There is a Kindred Redeemer who will free all from slavery and death and sin.

From this simple family who is dedicated to the Lord will come One who will redeem all humanity.

JONAH

A story about a man who ran away

The story of Jonah isn't like the ones we're used to telling. We're used to telling stories of people who accept a call to serve the Lord, frequently at significant risk and calamity to themselves. Stories like the Pioneers headed westward, giving up everything they had, walking through storms, hardships, and even death, to reach Zion. Or stories of people who, upon accepting the gospel, are asked to give up their homes and even their friends or family to choose the Lord. It could just be a simple story as well. Maybe not something so dramatic, but we're used to hearing stories of people who accept callings when the Lord calls them. We hear about people who proudly step up and boldly serve. It could be a person accepting a mission call. It could be the calling to be the Primary chorister or any calling in our ward or branch. When we tell the story about a calling from God, we talk about them accepting that call.

The story of Jonah is the opposite. The story of Jonah is about a man who runs away.

I love that the scriptures tell us stories about all kinds of life experiences, good and bad. The scriptures are not just about perfect people but about people who sin and make mistakes. They are about people who have questions, doubt, and plead to understand the Lord. They are stories of ordinary people, and they are right there in the pages of the Old Testament.

Growing up, I wasn't used to hearing about people who ran away. I certainly wasn't used to hearing about a prophet running away. And yet, here we are. That is the story of Jonah.

THE BEGINNING

It starts simply. The whole story is short. It's only four chapters that only take just a few minutes to read, but it will take a lifetime to digest all the meaning of this thought-provoking story. If you haven't read it recently, go back and read it. We'll go through it together, but this is one that you can easily read on your own.

Jonah Receives His Calling

"Now the word of the Lord. Came to Jonah, son of Amittai, saying, 'Go at once to Nineveh that great city and cry out against it for their wickedness has come up before me.' But Jonah set out to flee to Tarshish from the presence of the Lord" (NRSV, Jonah 1:1–3).

Before we get into this story about the prophet Jonah receiving a call and then fleeing, let's learn about the background of the people involved. This will make it easier to understand Jonah, and we will see that we might even have made the same choice if we had been in his shoes.

Nineveh and the Assyrians

God commands Jonah to go to a city called Nineveh. Nineveh is the capital city of the Assyrians (not Syrians with an S, Assyrians with an A). At the time, they are the superpower of the age. Nineveh is just outside what we think of as Mosel in modern-day Iraq. It is a thriving city, a mighty nation, and it is east of the land of Canaan. But this is not an ordinary city, and this is the capital of one of the most dominant empires the world had ever known.

The Assyrians were known for a few things. Yes, they were large and dominant. Yes, they were political. What set them apart was their ferocity as warriors. They were infamous for their standing army. This is one of the first times we see a professional military trained and focused on nothing but conquering. Unlike their neighbors who made up their armies from regular people, called into action only when war demanded, the Assyrians were pros.

The Assyrian army was more than just dominant—they inspired terror. One of the stone carvings that we still have from those days shows one of the horrific battle scenes. You may not want to read this, but the panel shows the captives having their tongues cut out before they were skinned alive. The Lachish Relief, a stone panel you can still see in the British Museum, has an inscription of King Sennacherib boasting of his victories: "Its inhabitants, young and old, I did not spare, and with their corpses, I filled the streets of the city."[1] A mission call to the Assyrians was the calling no one wanted.

Northern Kingdom of Israel

The Assyrians were tough on Israel and Jonah's hometown, Amittai. Let's do a quick recap on the northern and southern kingdoms. At this time, the Israelites have broken into two separate kingdoms. The ten tribes in the north are known as the Kingdom of Israel. There are two tribes in the south known as the Kingdom of Judah. Jerusalem is the capital in the south, and the capital city of the north is Samaria. (Yeah, you guessed it, that's where the name Samaritans come from that Jesus will talk about hundreds of years in the future.) Jonah is from Gath-Hepher, a town far to the north, just a few miles from the current city of Nazareth. That means Jonah is part of the Northern Kingdom. It is only a few short decades until the Assyrians completely take over and wipe out the Northern Kingdom. This is the time that we talk about the "lost ten tribes." The Assyrians destroy and take the tribes and cause complete their "losing." Jonah is from the north; these are his people.

---

1. Nineveh is one of the largest cities ever known in the world. It was over four or five square miles had an elaborate system of canals and hills. It had hundreds of thousands of inhabitants huge buildings. Nineveh is a superpower, but it's more important to see how truly large and scary it was. Reade, Julian, *Assyrian Sculpture* (British Museum Press, 2012), *56, 65–71) See also: Wall Relief,* Lachishhttps://www.britishmuseum.org/collection/object/W_1856–0909–35

The Assyrians aren't some obscure people group residing far away. They are the enemy that threatens to destroy his people, friends, and family. The evil of war that he has probably seen or been a part of can only be imagined. So, no, Nineveh will not have been on the top of Jonah's list of where he wants to go on his mission. And it wouldn't have been on the top of your list either.

(One other historical note that may show up in this story is the patron's goddess, Ninah, the goddess of the Assyrians, a great fish.[2] There's a big fish in this story, right? I bet that's important. Let's keep going).

THE STORY

Jonah hears the word of the Lord and is called to go to Nineveh. Instead of obeying, he turns and flees.

> But Jonah set out to flee to Tarshish from the presence of the Lord. He went down to Joppa and found a ship going to Tarshish; so he paid his fare and went on board, to go with them to Tarshish, away from the presence of the Lord. (NRSV, Jonah 1:3)

Jonah is going nowhere near Nineveh. Nineveh is far in the east, and he heads west now. Tarshish is believed to be in modern-day Spain, which means Jonah is running over 3,000 miles away.[3] He is going to the other end of the world.

There is one other detail about this introduction that is helpful in understanding Jonah. Anciently people believed in many gods. Each god had its area and people that it ruled. So, if you traveled to a different nation, say Egypt, some gods and goddesses ruled over those lands. For the ancients, it wasn't that there were or weren't other gods. It was who you worshiped. Also, those gods had power

---

2. "Nineveh," *Encyclopedia Judaica* (Gale Group, 2008).
3. Google maps, Jerusalem to Tarshish Spain. I had to estimate. It is far, really far. Dropping a pin from Jerusalem to Tartessos, Spain is over 3,000 miles or 4,800 kilometers.

in their region. So, when Jonah leaves the land of Canaan, the land Jehovah ruled, they would have seen it as Jonah fleeing from his god. Now, I know that's not how we think today, nor probably how Jonah as a prophet thought. But the story is ancient, like 3,000 years old, and that's how they would have seen Jonah fleeing. This story was told to those ancient people in a way they thought of the world around them. Jonah leaving and going far away is Jonah trying to get away from his God. It raises the question for us: Do we ever hide, thinking, "Maybe God won't notice me?" Do we ever flee in a vain attempt to get away, hoping we can leave behind something we hope to forget? Maybe we think, "God won't see me here. Maybe He won't notice or see what I'm doing."

Jonah flees. Jonah goes as far as ways he can by getting on a boat.

> But the Lord hurled a great wind upon the sea, and such a mighty storm came upon the sea that the ship threatened to break up. Then the mariners were afraid, and each cried to his God. They threw the cargo that was in the ship into the sea, to lighten it for them. Jonah, meanwhile, had gone down into the hold of the ship and had lain down, and was fast asleep. The captain came and said to him, "What are you doing sound asleep? Get up, call on your God! Perhaps the God will spare us a thought so that we do not perish. (NRSV, Jonah 1:4–6)

One of the repeating themes of this book is that God is aware of us. Here we see that God is completely aware of what Jonah is doing, and He's going to help him, prod him along a little, give him a little shove in the right direction. God is going to shake him up a bit, and it begins with a storm. Each of the sailors prays to each of their gods. The storm gets worse. Now they are really worried the ship is going to sink. They start throwing the cargo overboard. Panic hits. They are fearful they are going to die. The captain finds Jonah is asleep. Maybe he's not only literally asleep, but he's figuratively asleep, unaware of the reality God can see. The captain comes to him and demands action from Jonah: "What are you doing?

Why don't *you* pray? We are at critical here! Don't you realize we are all going to die?"

A Pause to Talk Style

Have we talked about the style, or genre, of this book yet? Let's do that right now. The style of the book of Jonah is satire.[4] Satire is a literary form that uses exaggeration to expose or criticize someone or something. Jonah is not "history but satire or parody, a ridiculous story that makes a serious point."[5] In this case, it's a little bit hard to see, but Jonah, the prophet, is the only one who doesn't believe. He's sleeping while they are all praying. This is not just any old storm. It is the storm-of-storms, the storm of the century—the biggest, meanest, fiercest storm. And where is the prophet? He is unaware; he is asleep. Later, we'll see when he actually does get to Nineveh (spoiler alert), everything is exaggerated. Nineveh isn't just big, but it is *huge*. The city is so large that it takes days to get around it and a day for Jonah to walk across it.[6] Because it's so big, everything in the story is in extra-large proportions—the biggest storm, the biggest fish, the most enormous army, the biggest city. Everything is exaggerated to make a more significant point: that the prophet is the one who doesn't believe the prophet is the one who flees. The satire will also emphasize one of our main themes, but you'll have to wait until the end. I don't want to spoil the story.

Now, back to the boat. The storm is threatening to drown all the passengers. The situation is beyond dire. It is an emergency. The captain comes and asks Jonah to pray (and I paraphrase): "What are you doing? Maybe you're the guy that's caused all this. How can

---

4. McKenzie, Steven L. *How to Read the Bible: History, Prophecy, Literature—Why Modern Readers Need to Know the Difference, and What It Means for Faith Today*, (New York: Oxford University Press, 2005), 1–21.

5 Ibid., 13.

6. I once walked halfway across Barcelona when my companion and I missed the train. It was a nice evening and we thought, "How far can it be?" We walked for hours and hours and only had to walk half the width of the city. There are millions of people living in Barcelona, and we eventually gave in and got a taxi.

you be sleeping?" It should strike us particularly odd that Jonah is sleeping. This is the storm-of-storms. No one could sleep through this storm. It is almost like Jonah is oblivious. He's not only physically unaware of what is going on, but he's also spiritually asleep. Or maybe he wants to ignore it. Perhaps he just wants to close his eyes, put his head under a pillow, and hope it will all go away.

There's probably a message in there for us.

> The sailors said to one another, "Come, let us cast lots, so that we may know on whose account this calamity has come upon us." So they cast lots, and the lot fell on Jonah. Then they said to him, "Tell us why this calamity has come upon us. What is your occupation? Where do you come from? What is your country? And of what people are you?" "I am a Hebrew," he replied. "I worship the Lord, the God of heaven, who made the sea and the dry land." Then the men were even more afraid, and said to him, "What is this that you have done!" For the men knew that he was fleeing from the presence of the Lord, because he had told them so. (NRSV, Jonah 1:7–10)

Jonah hasn't told him what's going on yet, so they know that someone must be to blame for such a miraculous, colossal storm. So, they cast lots. You've probably seen casting lots before. We even see it with Nephi and his brothers when they decide who will get the plates back from Laban (see 1 Nephi 4; Alma 20). Lots were thought to be a way that God could influence and tell them His intention. If you want to know what God decides and you live in ancient Israel, you cast lots. Now they are including God, so we know how this is going to go. And indeed, the lot falls on Jonah. You can almost feel them staring at him, incredulous and scared. "Why is this happening? Who are you? Where do you come from? Why are you doing this to us?" And then he confesses that he's a Hebrew and that it's God who makes the sea. Here we see that satire again. The sailors believe in the Lord. The sailors understand that he is fleeing from the Lord's presence. What did they do?

Then they said to him, "What shall we do to you, that the sea may quiet down for us?" For the sea was growing more and more tempestuous. He said to them, "Pick me up and throw me into the sea; then the sea will quiet down for you; for I know it is because of me that this great storm has come upon you." Nevertheless, the men rowed hard to bring the ship back to land, but they could not, for the sea grew more and more stormy against them. Then they cried out to the Lord, "Please, O Lord, we pray, do not let us perish on account of this man's life. Do not make us guilty of innocent blood; for you, O Lord, have done as it pleased you." So they picked Jonah up and threw him into the sea; and the sea ceased from its raging. Then, the men feared the Lord even more, and they offered a sacrifice to the Lord and made vows. (NRSV, Jonah 1:11–16)

And then, shockingly, the storm gets worse. The sailors, they believe, try to save Jonah, but Jonah says, "No, throw me overboard. I'm the one that caused it." Jonah knows what's happening. But the sailors try to save the boat. *They try to save him*!

(Quick aside: Remember this! The pagan sailors do everything they can to save the Hebrew prophet. It is key to understanding the theme of this story. *They try and save him*. Back to the story.)

The storm gets worse and worse. You can feel the panic. Then, suddenly they realize there's no other choice, and the crew throws Jonah overboard. "But the Lord provided a large fish to swallow up Jonah; and Jonah was in the belly of the fish three days and three nights" (Jonah 1:17).

Now, when all seems lost, the Lord does something *amazing*. He helps Jonah change his mind about fleeing. And God does this by having a big fish to swallow him up. Jonah is there for three days.

Usually, this is the part of the story that we focus on because we say, "Wow, this is amazing and crazy!" At this point in the story, someone in your ward starts the debate about it being a fish or a whale. Then your whole class devolves into the historical possibility if someone could live in a fish (or a whale) for three days.[7]

But this story is much more than a fish story. It is profoundly insightful about the nature of God that it is a shame that *this* is the part of the story we get stuck on. The big fish isn't even the main point of the story. Perhaps we turn to this detail because it is fantastic and hard to imagine. Maybe we remember this because it is one of the signs Christ gives the Pharisees about His death (see Matthew 12:38). We should take a minute to talk about this sign of the Savior. After all, this is one of the signs that Christ points to that say that the sign of Jonah is a sign of three days in a state of death, a state of the abyss and chaos.

The Sign of Jonah and Water

One of the ancient symbols that we sometimes overlook is the idea of water. Water is a symbol of both life and death. It represents life when it's life-giving like freshwater, like a stream or a river. Remember, these are desert people, so seeing a freshwater stream is the source of life. But saltwater is the opposite. The ocean is not our natural intended place. Instead, the sea is a place of chaos and destruction. If you think back to the Creation story in Genesis 1, watery chaos is how the Creation starts. It is from the chaos that God creates order and gives it life and purpose. From the churning water, Earth appears. There's the chaos, and in the calming of the waters, the creation of the Earth is separated. Water, especially seawater, is chaos, death, and disorder. It's the opposite of God. And so, Jonah, going into the water for three days, is going into chaos. He's going into death. From the depths of the abyss, we hear one of the greatest poems ever written.

---

7. In my mind I always think of the Disney movie *Pinocchio*, where Pinocchio and Geppetto are in the whale. Like Pinocchio, I imagine Jonah camping out inside with a little campfire, like hanging out in a little cave. I will never see Jonah quite the same. Now you won't see Jonah the same way either. Thanks a lot, Disney.

Then Jonah prayed to the Lord his God from the belly of the fish, saying,

"I called to the Lord out of my distress,
    and he answered me;
out of the belly of Sheol I cried,
    and you heard my voice.
You cast me into the deep,
    into the heart of the seas,
    and the flood surrounded me;
all your waves and your billows
    passed over me.
Then I said, 'I am driven away
    from your sight;
how shall I look again
    upon your holy temple?'
The waters closed in over me;
    the deep surrounded me;
weeds were wrapped around my head
    at the roots of the mountains.
I went down to the land
    whose bars closed upon me forever;
yet you brought up my life from the Pit,
    O Lord my God.
As my life was ebbing away,
    I remembered the Lord;
and my prayer came to you,
    into your holy temple.
Those who worship vain idols
    forsake their true loyalty.
But I with the voice of thanksgiving
    will sacrifice to you;
what I have vowed I will pay.
    Deliverance belongs to the Lord!"

Then the Lord spoke to the fish, and it spewed Jonah out upon the dry land (NRSV, Jonah 2:2–10)

From the depths of his greatest despair, from the darkness of the chaos, Jonah cries out to the Lord. From the anguish of his soul, he prays for salvation.

I love the way it starts: "I called to the Lord out of my distress out of the belly of Sheol. . . . I cried, 'You cast me into the deep . . . Into the heart of the seas, All the flood surrounded me, all your waves and your bellows crashed over me.'" You can feel it. Each phrase is like a wave, crashing over us, threatening to pull us under. The repeating sentence is that the ideas are swamped, overwhelmed, and overcome, just like Jonah. Sheol is the underworld, the place where spirits go after they die, and so he's there. He's in death. He's in despair, and they have overwhelmed him.

Reread it with me and feel the phrases, each level of desperation like a wave.

> You cast me into the deep, (*crash*)
>> into the heart of the seas, (*crash*)
>> and the flood surrounded me; (*the waves pick up now*)
> all your waves and your billows
>> passed over me. (*we are drowning*)

Then, he recounts how he needs the presence of the Lord. He looks to the temple, the place where God meets us.

> Then I said, 'I am driven away
>> from your sight;
> how shall I look again
>> upon your holy temple?'

He is ready to meet God, to have his presence. But not yet. He is still in despair.

> The waters closed in over me;
>> the deep surrounded me;
> weeds were wrapped around my head
>> at the roots of the mountains.
> I went down to the land
>> whose bars closed upon me forever;

yet you brought up my life from the Pit,
    O Lord my God.

He is truly at his lowest. He is nearing the point of giving up.

As my life was ebbing away,
    I remembered the Lord;
and my prayer came to you,
    into your holy temple.
Those who worship vain idols
    forsake their true loyalty.
But I with the voice of thanksgiving
    will sacrifice to you;
what I have vowed I will pay.
    Deliverance belongs to the Lord!"

At the point at which all is lost when his life is "ebbing away," he remembers his prayer. He recalls a time when he reached out to God. In the temple, where heaven and Earth meet, in the place where God's mercy seat is there to give Atonement, he offers up a sacrifice.

He is delivered. He is saved.

The fish spits up Jonah on dry ground.

Jonah's prayer from inside the depths is our prayer. When we can hold on no longer, we reach out to Him to hear us when we are at our end. When our anguish is so great, we can do nothing else but pray; we call to Him. From our humility, we turn to Him. He is there.

The temple is where heaven and Earth meet. In Moses's day, it was a tent called the Tent of Meeting (see Exodus 33:7). A special place where God's presence could be with His people. Remarkably, the special place of worship is a unique place where God can be with us. The temple replaced the tent, but the idea is the same. Jonah knows that there are times and places when God is incredibly close and especially aware of us. He calls out to God to remember that time, to remember Jonah. We can do the same. We can call out to Him to remember those sacred and holy moments when we knew He was there with us.

Headed to Nineveh

The story continues. Jonah is humbled and ready to obey the Lord. He is prepared to go to Nineveh. Here's the command again. "So Jonah set out and went to Nineveh, according to the word of the Lord. Now Nineveh was an exceedingly large city, a three days' walk across. Jonah began to go into the city, going a day's walk" (NRSV, Jonah 3:3–4).

The Lord gives His message again to Jonah: "Get up, go to Nineveh, that great city, and proclaim to it the message that I tell you!" And so Jonah goes. We are reminded that Nineveh is a giant city. With every step Jonah takes, we can feel the press and weight of it. It is so large because it is a contrast. The city is vast, and Jonah's message is very short.

It may be the shortest sermon ever given.

"Forty days more, and Nineveh shall be overthrown" (NRSV, Jonah 3:4).

That's Jonah's prophetic message. There's no beautiful insights, no singing of hymns, no long stories. There is no eloquent and moving sermon, no rousing speech. He says just a few words. In Hebrew, it is only five words. He says, "Clock is ticking. You're going to be destroyed." It's almost as if Jonah, despite the salvation and the redemption from the fish in his near-death, still is not very excited about preaching this. His short warning is a super brief message, yet to our utter shock, it works! The people of Nineveh repent.

When the news reached the king of Nineveh, he rose from his throne, removed his robe, covered himself with sackcloth, and sat in ashes. Then he had a proclamation made in Nineveh: "By the decree of the king and his nobles: No human being or animal, no herd or flock, shall taste anything. They shall not feed, nor shall they drink water. Human beings and animals shall be covered with sackcloth, and they shall cry mightily to God. All shall turn from their evil ways and from the violence that is in their hands. Who knows? God may relent and change his mind; he may turn from his fierce anger, so that we do not perish." (Jonah 3:6–9)

It starts with the king, who repents. He puts on sackcloth and ashes, symbols of repentance and remorse.[8] They are outward expressions of an inner feeling. We are so sad, realizing a loss, that nothing else has value. We do not wear our finest clothes, which reflect value. Instead, we are clothed in just sackcloth and ashes. It is in poverty in our souls that we repent and come before the Lord.

The king sends out a message to everyone, even the animals. Everyone is going to fast. Everyone's going to pray. To our shock, again, it works. The entire nation repents. These terrible, horrible people turn to God. "When God saw what they did, how they turned from their evil ways, God changed his mind about the calamity that he had said he would bring upon them; and he did not do it" (NRSV, Jonah 3:10).

Here in the last verse of chapter 3 we start to see the message of this amazing little book. When the people, the evil and terrible people of Nineveh, hear the message of God, they repent, and, shockingly, God *forgives them*. It should be startling to us. These people who have been torturing their enemies, destroying nations, change. This nation is not Israelite. This nation does not know the Lord. Maybe even more shocking is that God loves them, too.

Is that the message of the story? Yes, of course. The story is that God loves all of His children. And what of Jonah? The story doesn't end here. The Lord has more to say to us. The story is about Jonah. So how does he respond to this amazing miracle to this turn of events that these people turn to the Lord?

---

8. In 2 Samuel 3:31, David mourns the death of Abner, the commander of Saul's army, in sackcloth and ashes. Jacob does the same, following what he thought was the death of Joseph (see Genesis 37:34). The tradition continues into the time of Christ with Matthew 11:21.

But this was very displeasing to Jonah, and he became angry. He prayed to The Lord and said, "O Lord! Is not this what I said while I was still in my own country? That is why I fled to Tarshish at the beginning; for I knew that you are a gracious God and merciful, slow to anger, and abounding in steadfast love, and ready to relent from punishing. And now, O Lord, please take my life from me, for it is better for me to die than to live." (NRSV, Jonah 4:1–3)

Shockingly, Jonah is not pleased that the people repent. He becomes angry and tells the Lord, "I I knew what would happen! This is why I left. I knew that you were merciful. I knew that they would be blessed. I knew that you would love them."

He quotes the most quoted scripture in the Old Testament: "I know that you were gracious and merciful. You are slow to anger and abounding in steadfast love." This quote comes from Exodus 34:6 and is how God chooses to describe himself in the Old Testament. We may not think that we might say, "No, the God of the Old Testament seems harsh. He likes punishing the wicked. There are curses and plagues. There are wars and political upheavals." Yet, in the story of the Old Testament, God chooses to describe Himself. This verse is how He does it. He tells us of His most poignant attributes, His characteristics. How does God describe Himself? Merciful. Slow to anger. Abounding in covenant faithfulness and steadfast love. And ready to relent from punishing.

Jonah knows this about the Lord as well. The character of God is why Jonah didn't want to go. Now we understand why he fled. Because Jonah hates them, he cannot bear to see them live. He wants to see them punished, and yet he knows that God loves them too. In the most truthful of admissions, Jonah tells us what he couldn't bear, that God loves everyone, even our enemies.

"And now, O Lord, please take my life from me, for it is better for me to die than to live." And the Lord said, 'Is it right for you to be angry?'" (Jonah 4:4).

Jonah is so upset. This is what he had feared all along. He says, "Kill me. I cannot bear this." And the Lord chastens Jonah: "Is it right for you to be angry?" Is it okay to be angry that a people repented? It is okay for us to feel that way when bad people change? The story of Jonah reminds us that God loves all His children, even those we think are our enemies.

Remember the sailors, who did everything they could to save Jonah? Can you see the irony now? These pagans were willing to risk the ship and even their lives for this stranger. Jonah, on the other hand, wouldn't even share a message. What does that tell us about how we see others? Are our enemies worthy of saving?

> Then Jonah went out of the city and sat down east of the city, and made a booth for himself there. He sat under it in the shade, waiting to see what would become of the city. The Lord God appointed a bush, and made it come up over Jonah, to give shade over his head, to save him from his discomfort; so Jonah was very happy about the bush. But when dawn came up the next day, God appointed a worm that attacked the bush, so that it withered. When the sun rose, God prepared a sultry east wind, and the sun beat down on the head of Jonah so that he was faint and asked that he might die. He said, "It is better for me to die than to live." (Jonah 4:5–8)

The book ends with this final story—this object lesson that the Lord tries to teach Jonah and us. Jonah goes to the east side of the city and makes himself a little tent. He just sits there and waits and watches for, what he hopes, is the divine destruction of the people of Nineveh. Like a twisted fireworks show, Jonah waits for Nineveh to fall. While he remains there, God makes a small bush that comes and gives him a bit of shade. It's hot, it's desert, and so Jonah appreciates the little shrub. He's very connected, almost satirically connected, to the bush.

The next day, God creates a worm that attacks the bush, and the bush dies. Without protection, the wind and the sun beat down on Jonah. He's hot, frustrated, and miserable without the bush. Remember the satire here—the exaggeration—that he could just die. He says it's just better for him to die than to live. He's so upset. He is almost like a child throwing a temper tantrum.

The Lord himself gives us the moral of the story in the last few verses.

> But God said to Jonah, "Is it right for you to be angry about the bush?" And he said, "Yes, angry enough to die." Then the Lord said, "You are concerned about the bush, for which you did not labor and which you did not grow; it came into being in a night and perished in a night. And should I not be concerned about Nineveh, that great city, in which there are more than a hundred and twenty thousand persons who do not know their right hand from their left, and also many animals?" (Jonah 4:9–11)

God uses this object lesson to teach Jonah and us. God loves everyone. Jonah didn't create the bush. God did. Jonah did not create the worm either. Jonah didn't cause any of the good things or the bad things to happen. God did. We learn here that God loves everyone.

In the final sentence of the final verse of the final chapter of the small book of Jonah, we learn the stupidity of prejudice. We see how hatred of others, even our enemies, is ridiculous. God teaches us that our bigotry toward others is foolish. God asks Jonah a question, one that we should ask ourselves (and this is the point of the whole story). Doesn't God love all those people? Even their animals? God loves His creations. God loves His children. God loves our enemies and the people who don't deserve it, the people who have hurt us, and the people who never seem to do the right things and get every break. He loves them, too. He loves all of them, *just like He loves us.* So, we are left to ponder the message of Jonah: What happens when God loves everyone?

What of this story of Jonah? What did you learn about a man who, when called, ran away? When our prejudices and feelings make us less forgiving, what will we do? What does the story tell us to do when we don' like the people we serve with, the family we are "stuck with"? When our enemies are blessed, when someone who has harmed us returns to the Lord, will we sit on the hillside and hope they fail?

When we are faced with our own feelings of bigotry and hatred, remember the story of Jonah, the man who ran away.

LAST THOUGHTS

Growing up, I thought that scripture stories only had perfect examples. I learned that the opposite is true. Real people fill their pages. The scriptures invite me to look deeper and see how God works with imperfect people. When I dive deeply into their pages, I see sinners, failures, and doubters. I also see miracles and wonders. I see the Lord in every page, working to make these imperfect people better.

I see myself.

One of the strengths of the Old Testament is how real the people are. We see these people's mistakes, failings, and imperfections. They doubt, fail, and sin. They also have glorious moments of success. They trust in God, and He makes them more than they ever thought possible. In them I can see myself, and I can have hope that I, too, in Christ, can succeed.

Elder Jeffrey R. Holland said, "So be kind regarding human frailty—your own as well as that of those who serve with you in a Church led by volunteer, mortal men and women. Except in the case of His only perfect Begotten Son, imperfect people are all God has ever had to work with. That must be terribly frustrating to Him, but He deals with it. So should we."

In times of failure and doubt, turn to the heroes of the Old Testament. Remember Abraham and Isaac, Rebekah, Jacob, and Esau. When you are unsure you are up to a task, turn to Gideon and Deborah, and remember that the Lord is on your side. When struggles overwhelm you, call on the strength of Moses, Miriam, and Aaron to lighten your load. Serve and obey like Ruth and Boaz, letting each day welcome the Lord into your life. The Lord love us. He loves you. Like those heroes of old, He will be with you to strengthen you and perform wonders.

In the words of the prophet Isaiah:

> You are my servant,
> I have chosen you and not cast you off;
> do not fear, for I am with you,
> do not be afraid, for I am your God;
> I will strengthen you, I will help you,
> I will uphold you with my victorious right hand.
> (NRSV, Isaiah 41:9–10)

BIBLIOGRAPHY

Alter, Robert. 2019. *The Art of Bible Translation*. Princeton: Princeton University Press.

_____. 2011. *The Art of Biblical Narrative*. Philadelphia: Basic Books.

Auerbach, Erich. 1968. *Mimesis: The Representation of Reality in Western Literature*. Translated by Willard R. Trask. Princeton, NJ: Princeton University Press.

Billauer, Barbara P. 2004. "Moses, The Tutmoses and the Exodus." (SSRN) April. SSRN: https://ssrn.com/abstract=2429297 .

Brown, Kent S. 1998. "The Exodus Pattern in the Book of Mormon." *From Jerusalem to Zarahemla: Literary and Historical Studies of the Book of Mormon* (Religious Studies Center, Brigham Young University) 75–98.

Butler, T. 1979. "An Anti-Moses Tradition." *JSOT* 12: 9–15.

Childs, Bevard. 1970. "Moses's Slaying in the Theology of the Two Testaments." *Biblical Theology in Crisis*, 1970.

Driver, F. Brown, and C. Briggs. 2004. *The Brown-Driver-Briggs Hebrew and English Lexicon*. Boston, MA: Houghton, Mifflin and Company.

Gaskill, Alonzo L. 2003. *The Lost Language of Symbolism*. Salt Lake City: Deseret Book.

Hayes, Christine. 2012. *Introduction to the Bible*. New Haven and London: Yale University Press.

Hoffmeier, James K. 1999. *Israel in Egypt.* Oxford: Oxford University Press.

Holland, Jeffrey R. 2013. "Lord, I Believe." *Liahona.*

McConkie, Bruce R. 1985. *A New Witness for the Articles of Faith.* Salt Lake City: Desert Book.

McKenzie, Stephen L. 2005. *How to the Read the Bible: History, Prophecy, Literature—Why Modern Readers Need to Know the Difference, and What It Means for Faith Today.* New York: Oxford University Press.

Nelson, Russell M. 2020. "Let God Prevail." *Liahona.*

Nelson, Russell M. 2021. "The temple is Your Spiritual Foundation." *Liahona Magazine.*

Sailhamer, John H. 1992. *The Pentateuch as Narrative.* Grand Rapids, MI: Zondervan Publishing House.

Sarna, Nahum M. 2015. *Understanding Genesis.* New York: The Jewish Theological Seminary of America.

n.d. *The Holy Bible.*

Trenchard, Warren C. 2003. *A Concise Dictionary of the Words in the Greek New Testament and The Hebrew Bible.* Cambridge: Cambridge University Press.

ABOUT THE AUTHOR

Lori Denning is a scripture nerd. She holds a bachelor's degree in biblical studies from Multnomah University, where she studied Hebrew and the Bible and was awarded highest honors. She holds a master's degree in theology from Gonzaga University.

Sister Denning has taught Gospel Doctrine classes, as well as classes in the Church Educational System. She has a popular vlog, *The Bible Brief,* introducing books of the Bible to a wide audience. She also hosts a podcast, *:20 Minute Scriptorian*, which covers the *Come, Follow Me* curriculum. Her passion is sharing the gospel of Jesus Christ through His scriptures.

Lori served a mission in Barcelona, Spain, and currently resides in South Jordan, Utah.